INVESTMENT GOVERNANCE FOR FIDUCIARIES

Michael E. Drew and Adam N. Walk

CFA Institute
Research
Foundation

Statement of Purpose

The CFA Institute Research Foundation is a not-for-profit organization established to promote the development and dissemination of relevant research for investment practitioners worldwide.

CFA®, Chartered Financial Analyst®, and GIPS® are just a few of the trademarks owned by CFA Institute. To view a list of CFA Institute trademarks and the Guide for the Use of CFA Institute Marks, please visit our website at www.cfainstitute.org.

This publication is designed to provide accurate and authoritative information in regard to the subject matter covered. It is sold with the understanding that the publisher is not engaged in rendering legal, accounting, or other professional service. If legal advice or other expert assistance is required, the services of a competent professional should be sought.

Cover photo credit: Roland Shainidze Photography / Moment / Getty Images

ISBN 978-1-944960-69-8

Disclosure

The authors of this book are partners of Stonechat Capital. The views in the book are the authors' views. Such opinions are subject to change without notice. This publication has been distributed for educational purposes only and should not be considered as investment or legal advice or a recommendation of any particular security, strategy, or investment product. Information contained herein has been obtained from sources believed to be reliable but is not guaranteed.

This publication contains a general discussion of investment governance and should not be used or relied upon as a substitute for professional advice or as a basis for formulating business decisions. The analysis does not take into consideration any particular investor's financial circumstances, objectives, or risk tolerance. Investments discussed may not be suitable for all investors.

Nothing contained herein is intended to constitute accounting, governance, legal, tax, securities, or investment advice or an opinion regarding the appropriateness of any investment or a solicitation of any type, and nothing in this book should be acted upon as such.

Biographies

Michael E. Drew is managing partner of Stonechat Capital; a director of Drew, Walk & Co.; and a professor of finance at Griffith University. He is a financial economist specializing in the areas of investment governance, pension plan design, and outcome-oriented investing. Professor Drew's research has been published in leading practitioner journals, including the *Journal of Pension Economics and Finance*, the *Journal of Portfolio Management*, and the *Journal of Retirement*. He has been invited to make submissions and to testify before numerous committees, including the US Department of Labor and the SEC joint hearing on target-date funds. Professor Drew serves as a specialist member of the QSuper Investment Committee and is a member of the Investment Advisory Board of the Petroleum Fund of *Timor-Leste* (East Timor). He received his PhD in economics from the University of Queensland, is an Accredited Investment Fiduciary Analyst®, and is a Life Member of FINSIA, the Financial Services Institute of Australasia.

Adam N. Walk is a partner of Stonechat Capital; a director of Drew, Walk & Co.; and an adjunct professor at the University of Notre Dame–Australia. He is a financial economist specializing in the areas of investment governance, pension finance, and investments. Dr Walk's research has been published in the *Journal of Portfolio Management* and the *Journal of Retirement*. He serves as an alternate director of Rest and adviser to the Group Capital and Investment Committee at RACQ Group, is a board member of the Archdiocesan Development Fund of the Roman Catholic Archdiocese of Brisbane, and is deputy chair and a trustee of Campion College Australia. Dr Walk received his PhD in financial economics from Griffith University, Queensland, Australia. He is an Accredited Investment Fiduciary Analyst® and a Certified Investment Management Analyst® designee.

Contents

CE Qualified Activity   CFA Institute   This publication qualifies for 5 CE credits under the guidelines of the CFA Institute Continuing Education Program.

Foreword

To say that the financial well-being of hundreds of millions of people around the globe rests on the performance of the tens of trillions of dollars held in funds with long-term investment horizons is not hyperbole. Whether these assets belong to defined-benefit or defined-contribution retirement plans, endowments or foundations, or other special-purpose funds, and whether the funds are large or small, public or private—virtually all of us have a stake in their successful investment. But who are the people who oversee these investments, and what are their credentials?

According to the Greenwich Roundtable, the United States alone is home to more than 100,000 asset pools with investment horizons exceeding 10 years and a total of more than US$14 trillion invested in just the largest pools. (The numbers are much greater, of course, on a global level.) Moreover, according to estimates, in the United States alone, more than 500,000 individuals sit on the governing boards of these funds and another 500,000 people have responsibilities for investing the assets.[1] We often hear news about the boards of large public pension funds. Left unmentioned are the defined-contribution plans of small companies or the capital improvement funds of local religious institutions. Although the large funds have greater societal impact, how well the people overseeing modestly sized funds carry out their duties matters just as much to the funds' beneficiaries as the decisions of the board of, for example, the huge California Public Employees Retirement System matter to its many plan participants and other stakeholders.

Billions of dollars are spent annually on the services of investment managers, consultants, recordkeepers, and auditors—all with the intent of keeping the system functioning smoothly and effectively. Compared with the immense resources devoted to directly implementing the investments of these asset pools, disappointingly little time and money is spent on one of the fundamental underpinnings of successful investment programs: sound investment governance.

Most individuals who serve on fund governing boards and investment committees were selected for reasons other than their explicit understanding of investments and investment governance issues. Virtually all wish to do well in their roles, but most initially come to the table without the knowledge required to function confidently. From an educational perspective, these people often receive little attention. Typically, they learn on the job. Even

---

[1]See McMenamin (2015).

for those board or committee members who proactively want to become better informed, resources are limited. The few investment governance materials that are available usually address narrow legal issues. With some exceptions, largely missing are practical discussions intended to help those people charged with high-level oversight of pools of invested assets do better at their jobs.

Facing this dearth of educational resources, *Investment Governance for Fiduciaries* by Michael Drew and Adam Walk is a welcome addition to the investment governance library. With their grounding in the "real world," combined with their academic training, the authors' backgrounds make them highly qualified to address this topic. They put their professional knowledge and experience to use in developing a simple and straightforward approach to fulfilling the role of fund "fiduciaries"—those people with investment program oversight.

To the layperson, the role of an investment fiduciary may seem like an overwhelming task. The many decisions that are involved and the weight of the responsibilities are daunting. Whereas the fiduciaries of large funds have the budgets to hire outside consultants and legal experts, the fiduciaries of small funds may be left to rely on their own knowledge and good intentions. For either group, however, authors Drew and Walk provide a simple and logical framework around which investment fiduciaries can organize and evaluate their own governance practices and make structural improvements.

Drew and Walk define investment governance as ". . . the effective use of resources—people, policies, processes, and systems—by an individual or governing body (the fiduciary or agent) seeking to fulfill a fiduciary duty to a principal (or beneficiary) in addressing an underlying investment challenge." The authors identify five components of this investment governance framework: setting objective(s), policy, execution and resources, implementation, and superintending (or overseeing). Within their discussion of each component, the authors do an excellent job of explaining the key aspects, delving into more nuanced considerations, and providing helpful recommendations. The bibliography gives readers the opportunity to do further research on various aspects of investment governance.

I highly recommend this book not only to all investment fiduciaries but also to the consultants, investment managers, recordkeepers, lawyers, and anyone else who works with the unsung and dedicated people who keep our invested assets safe and productively invested.

Jeff Bailey
Finance Lecturer, University of Minnesota
Former Senior Director, Benefits, Target Corporation

Preface

This book is the product of 25 years or so of professional experience across industry and academia, during which we have worked—mostly with each other—on matters of investment governance. Our professional collaboration began when we worked as the senior investment *governance* officers of a pension fund that offered both defined-benefit and defined-contribution plans and for which the investment function was substantially delegated to external parties (some of which were related). The investment governance ecosystem in which this fund existed was formative to our views on the subject. We began as staff acting as gatekeepers for lay fiduciaries who were faced with the best (and worst) the industry had to offer during the best and worst of times (including the global financial crisis of 2007–2008).

Now, as independent consultants and fiduciaries, we see the same issues from a slightly different perspective. Some of our views have been confirmed, others challenged. What has become patently obvious to us is that *good process* has *common elements* and (near) *universal application* irrespective of the fiduciary role and the underlying investment challenge.

The intent of this book is to share with fiduciaries ideas that may help them fulfill their duties to beneficiaries (and other stakeholders). Asset consultants and investment managers may find it useful in establishing their credibility among, and pitching their services to, fiduciaries. The book was primarily written for fiduciaries, however, who, in our experience, take seriously the underappreciated role for which they are appointed (many on a *pro bono* basis). Some of the words may grate on the nerves of various industry players because we challenge them to follow the advice of Charles D. Ellis, CFA, in his well-known *Financial Analysts Journal* paper "The Winners' Game" (2011): Prioritize the *values* of the profession (i.e., serve those it should be serving) over the *economics* [original emphasis] of the business (its own commercial interests).

For those readers who are time poor—most of you we suspect—we have added at the end of each chapter a list of "points for reflection." Those who want to quickly determine whether this book is relevant to them may wish to begin there. If you can answer most of these points in the affirmative, you are likely well on your way to investment governance best practice. If you don't understand what the points are asking you, the answer is in the negative, or the answer is "somebody else does that," you might want to delve into the book a little farther.

MED and ANW
Brisbane, Australia
February 2019

Acknowledgments

We thank Chris Anast, Michael Block, Josh Cohen, Catherine Collinson, Lee Freitag, Brad Holzberger, J. Richard Lynch, Lew Minsky, Karl Morris, Danielle Press, Sonya Sawtell-Rickson, Stacy Schaus, David Skinner, Pauline Vamos, and Sue Walton for generously providing their thoughts on investment governance—"in their own words"—contained in this book.

The following people, although they might not know it, have had an influence on how we think about investments in general and investment governance in particular: Keith Ambachtsheer, Carl Bacon, Philip Booth, Tom Brakke, Stephen Brown, Gordon Clark, Charles Ellis, Marty Gruber, Philippe Jorion, François-Serge Lhabitant, Olivia Mitchell, Ashby Monk, Alicia Munnell, David Neal, Adrian Orr, Bill Sharpe, Larry Siegel, Frank Sortino, David Spaulding, Roger Urwin, Geoff Warren, Russ Wermers, and Dariusz Wójcik. Their insights are formally acknowledged throughout the book.

The following colleagues have made the years of experience that went into this book more rewarding and, at times, entertaining. We acknowledge Mary Adams, Blaine Aikin, David Andrew, Mark Arnold, Kevin Bailey, Hamish Bain, Dan Baxter, Lorraine Berends, Barry Bicknell, Kate Bromley, Drew Carrington, Kim Chew, (the late) Mark Christensen, Stephen Christie, Adam Clements, Chris Condon, Andrew Cooke, Jeremy Cooper, Glenn Crane, Laurence Crawley, Dan Daugaard, Ollie De Castro, Jane Dharam, Aaron Drew, Jeremy Duffield, Jeff Falvey, Simon Fenwick, Anne Finney, Ross Fowler, Michael Furey, Sandy Grant, Philip Greenheld, Steve Hackworth, Scott Healy, Gary Humphrys, Walter Ivessa, ("Slammin'") Sam Kendall, (the late) Don Kofoed, Allan Layton, Colin Martin, Michael Matthews, Russell McCrory, Shane McGarry, Len McKeering, Doug McTaggart, Con Michalakis, Beth Mohle, Claire Molinari, (the late) Tony Naughton, Scott Pappas, Mark Pearce, Michael Pennisi, John Polichronis, James Power, Deborah Ralston, Evan Reedman, Troy ("the Rhino") Rieck, Adriaan Ryder, Jim Sia, Kulwant Singh-Pangly, Jason Smith, Nick Stewart, Nigel Stewart, Sh'vorn Sumner, Tørres Trovik, Paul Umbrazunas, Nick Vamvakas, Rosemary Vilgan, Chris Wells, (the late) Bob ("Mr. Bob") Wilson, Jane Wilson, Steve Wilson, and Kathryn Young.

To our much-admired academic collaborators, Anup Basu, Robert Bianchi, Jacqueline Drew, Mike Evans, John Fan, Jon Stanford, Madhu Veeraraghavan, Jason West, Tim Whittaker, and Osei Wiafe, we give thanks for sharing your space on the academic treadmill with us.

We thank the CFA Institute Research Foundation for its support and encouragement. In particular, we would like to sincerely thank Bud Haslett, executive director of the CFA Institute Research Foundation, and Larry Siegel, the Gary P. Brinson Director of Research at the CFA Institute Research Foundation, for seeing this project from three pages of ideas to the current volume. We also thank the editorial staff and Jessica Critzer for their kind assistance.

A special vote of thanks goes out to Jo Butler and Grace Cooke, our patient practice managers who faithfully make the trains run on time (well, most of the time).

Finally, we would like to extend our sincere gratitude to our respective families—Jacqueline, Nicholas, and Alexander Drew and Megan Walk—for their love and support. Without it, we would be lost.

1. Why Investment Governance?

"The finance sector *devotes too little attention to* the search for new investment opportunities and *the stewardship of existing ones*, and far too much to secondary-market dealing in existing assets."

—John Kay (2016); italics added

The word "governance" is increasingly heard and written about in modern times. *Global governance* is a question that exercises the minds of national governments when attending multilateral meetings on subjects ranging from trade to climate change. Effective *corporate governance* is what boards of directors attempt to provide for the corporations they represent and is the standard to which investors and activists increasingly hold them. In this book, we focus our attention on the rapidly growing field of *investment governance*.

Before proceeding, it is important to outline exactly what we mean by *investment governance*:

> Investment governance refers to the effective use of resources—people, policies, processes, and systems—by an individual or governing body (the fiduciary or agent) seeking to fulfill a fiduciary duty to a principal (or beneficiary) in addressing an underlying investment challenge.

Let's consider each of the elements of this definition in turn. First, the functional *purpose* of investment governance is to address an underlying investment issue. This investment challenge depends on a range of factors, discussed in detail in Chapters 2 and 3, that deal with, respectively, investment beliefs and investment objectives. Importantly, throughout this book the investment issues we discuss are usually found in one of three contexts: (1) defined-contribution (DC) plans, (2) defined-benefit (DB) plans, or (3) endowments and foundations (E&Fs). Why we chose these three contexts will become apparent by the time the reader has completed this chapter. At this point, we note only that each context brings with it a different set of investment beliefs and objectives and a different institutional setting.

Second, investment governance involves a *relationship* between the fiduciary (the agent) and the beneficiary (or principal), on whose behalf the fiduciary discharges legal obligations, customarily known as "fiduciary duties."[2] Agency theory, although not formalized until the 20th century, was

---

[2]The specific legal obligations of fiduciaries vary by jurisdiction. For this book, we are defining it broadly as a relationship of trust and confidence involving the highest standards of care, loyalty, good faith, and prudence. Fiduciary duty also usually involves duties of confidentiality and disclosure.

foreshadowed in 1776 by Adam Smith (1937) when he wrote of joint-stock companies:[3]

> The directors of such companies, however, being the managers rather of other people's money than of their own, it cannot well be expected, that they should watch over it with the same anxious vigilance with which the partners in a private copartnery frequently watch over their own. Like the stewards of a rich man, they are apt to consider attention to small matters as not for their master's honor, and very easily give themselves a dispensation from having it. Negligence and profusion, therefore, must always prevail, more or less, in the management of the affairs of such a company. (p. 700)

Fiduciary duty exists to allow specialization and to ensure, as far as possible, that "anxious vigilance" is applied on behalf of the beneficiary (the principal), thereby minimizing agency risk.[4] As the reader will see when considering our three contexts—DC plans, DB plans, and E&Fs—the ability of fiduciaries to understand the interests of myriad principals can make practical investment governance a challenge. For example, in a DC plan with 500,000 beneficiaries, how does a fiduciary fulfill her fiduciary duty? We grapple with this question as we discuss investment objectives in Chapter 3.

In their own words ...

"The QSuper Board considers investment governance as a crucial and fundamental cornerstone in the fulfillment of its fiduciary duty."

—*Karl Morris, Chair, QSuper*

Although the potential for divergent interests between the fiduciary and beneficiary is certainly of concern in investment governance, another potential divergence of interest relates to asset (or investment) *consultants* and their

---

[3]Although Smith is known by many as an economist, when considering a duty to others, recall that he was a moral philosopher first and foremost; see Smith's *The Theory of Moral Sentiments* ([1759] 2016). For the moral grounding for fiduciary duties, readers are directed to Young (2007) for an overview.

[4]Agency risk is broadly defined as the risk of the agent prioritizing his or her divergent interests over those of the principal. More technically, Jensen and Meckling (1976) summarized agency risk as the "divergence between the agent's decisions and those decisions which would maximize the welfare of the principal" (p. 5). In the same paper, the authors defined agency costs as "the sum of: (1) the monitoring expenditures by the principal; (2) the bonding expenditures by the agent; and, (3) the residual loss" (pp. 5–6).

sometimes-conflicted role in advising fiduciaries on matters of both investment policy and investment selection. We turn to this issue later in this chapter when we introduce our investment process and what we call the *fiduciary line*.

The final element of our definition of investment governance relates to the need to effectively use resources to properly carry out governance. Regulators and other interested parties are keen to ensure that the resources used in governance are appropriate in light of the underlying investment challenge.[5] As complexity increases, for example, a concomitant increase in the quality and/or quantity of resources used to address the investment issue would be expected. For example, the interaction between the role of DC plan fiduciaries and their capabilities is widely debated. Such fiduciaries are often appointed to represent individual beneficiaries by a particular beneficiary group—for example, a union official representing police officers; however, an additional requirement is that each fiduciary be able to contribute to the governance of complex investment portfolios. Thus, tension may exist between the fiduciary's role and his or her capability.

Can we make a distinction between *investment governance* expertise and *investment* expertise? As the reader will see, we believe such a distinction exists and that lay fiduciaries—for whom the fiduciary aspect of their role is prioritized over their capabilities—are appropriate in certain circumstances.

Before turning to the central concern of this chapter—why investment governance is important—some other terms need to be defined. A term that is used widely by fiduciaries is "stewardship," especially in the context of not-for-profit organizations, such as E&Fs. For such entities, fiduciaries are required to trade off the achievement of objectives today (say, fulfilling the foundation's charitable purpose with respect to current needs) with future achievement (responding to future needs). Successfully achieving this balance is what we would describe as *good stewardship*, and it requires effective investment governance in cases in which investable assets are involved. Although effective investment governance is necessary to good stewardship, it is not sufficient. The steward's remit is broader than investment-related decision making.

---

[5]For example, Australia's prudential regulator, the Australian Prudential Regulation Authority, requires pension plans (or what in Australia are called "superannuation funds") to have an investment governance framework "appropriate to the size, business mix and complexity" of the regulated entity's operations (APRA 2013a).

The Significance of Investment Governance

Effective investment governance enables good stewardship. For this reason, it should be of interest to all fiduciaries, no matter the size of the pool of assets they handle or the nature of the beneficiaries. The importance of effective investment governance for various types of organizations is why we consider governance in three contexts. The elements of effective investment governance apply universally.

A philosophical or principle-based argument reveals the importance of investment governance, but in addition, certain secular trends make raising standards even more urgent. These trends are related and, at the same time, self-reinforcing.

First, the task is of increasing importance because of the sheer weight of money. Global pension assets in 22 major markets were estimated at US$36.4 trillion at the end of 2016—or 62% of the GDP of these countries—having grown 4.3% during the previous year (Willis Towers Watson 2017a). Although this number is large, the World Economic Forum (2017) estimated that the retirement savings gap—the gap between retirement assets and the liabilities they exist to finance—was US$70 trillion in 2015, and the gap is predicted to be around US$400 trillion by 2050 (admittedly, forecasts over such a long time horizon are susceptible to substantial error). Importantly, these retirement gap figures relate only to the eight largest established retirement systems; the true asset shortfall is much larger.[6]

In addition to, it is hoped, closing the gap, some factors complicate the task of managing the existing retirement assets (World Economic Forum 2017).[7] Such factors are as follows:

- *Increasing life expectancies and lower birth rates*—Relatively static retirement ages mean that whatever savings are generated are required to finance increasingly longer retirements. High *dependency ratios* (i.e., the number of dependents birth to 14 years old and over the age of 65 to the total population age 15 to 64) mean that public finances will be increasingly unable to make up for any inadequacy in private retirement savings.

---

[6]A growing body of literature addresses the gaping difference between retirement liabilities (or planned/hoped-for consumption) and the assets held to back them. For example, see the work of Olivia S. Mitchell, University of Pennsylvania (e.g., Mitchell, Maurer, and Hammond 2014); Alicia H. Munnell, Boston College (e.g., Clark, Munnell, and Orszag 2006; Munnell and Sass 2008; Ellis, Eschtruth, and Munnell 2014); and Laurence B. Siegel for the CFA Institute Research Foundation (e.g., Siegel 2015; Sexauer and Siegel 2017).
[7]Interestingly, Natixis Global Asset Management (2017), in its Global Retirement Index, identifies (p. 7) poor governance as a "key driving force" behind the "below-average performance" of the BRIC countries (Brazil, Russia, India, and China).

- *Lack of easy access to pensions*—Not all individuals have access to pensions. If these individuals were included, the retirement savings gap would be even larger than official estimates.

- *Long-term low growth environment*—The consensus (to be discussed) is that investment returns are unlikely to be able to make up for inadequate savings rates.

- *Low levels of financial literacy*—Limited financial literacy leads to poor financial decisions, increasing the threat to retirement savings.

- *Inadequate savings rates*—Savings rates are presently insufficient to produce an adequate *income-replacement ratio* (a person's gross income after retirement divided by his or her gross income before retirement) in retirement. The World Economic Forum (2017) estimated that income-replacement ratios need to be increased between double and triple current levels (i.e., from around 5% to 10%–15%) to close the gap.

- *High degree of individual responsibility to manage pensions*—The responsibility for retirement security remains with the individual in DC plans, but the investment management function is often provided by a financial services firm. To the extent that a financial services firm acts (or ought to act) on behalf of the individual, the importance of the investment governance issues we discuss increases.

In addition to the issues surrounding retirement savings, E&Fs (including charities) remain an important part of civil society and a valuable source of funds and services for certain sectors in the economy (e.g., education, social services). The tax benefits (usually) extended to these organizations, and the public policy consequences of their failure, mean that the public has an interest in how E&Fs are governed.

Second, this "weight-of-money" argument has been reinforced by the *rising standards of behavior* expected of financial service providers. Since the financial crisis of 2007–2008, the financial sector's place in the economy, its methods, and its ethics have been (rightly, in many cases) under scrutiny. In parallel, and fed by the expectations for higher standards, has come the rise of a type of investing known as "socially responsible investing" or several other more-or-less synonymous names: "ethical investing" or "investing that takes into account environmental, social, and governance (ESG) factors." These tendencies have had the effect of shining a light on the way financial resources are governed.

Third, and finally, generally higher expectations have fed into *regulation and activism*. Perhaps the most prominent example of *proposed* new regulation is the US Department of Labor Fiduciary Rule, which set out to hold those providing retirement investment advice to employee benefit plans to a fiduciary standard.[8] The proposed Fiduciary Rule explicitly stated the rationale for the imposition of this standard:

> Under this regulatory structure, fiduciary status and responsibilities are central to protecting the public interest in the integrity of retirement and other important benefits, many of which are tax-favored.[9]

Thus, although the Fiduciary Rule never came into being, it shows the momentum toward codifying heightened standards to protect the public interest.

Furthermore, nongovernmental entities have begun, ostensibly in the public interest, to hold fiduciaries to these heightened standards. Such entities include global pension funds, activist investors, and issue-specific activist groups (e.g., those working to eliminate the use of fossil fuels or the sale of tobacco). For example, in the United Kingdom, increasing numbers of pension funds, citing "both ethical and financial reasons for reducing exposure" (Mooney 2017), are divesting from fossil fuel producers. Data from the activist group 350.org suggest that some 700 investors have committed to "cutting their exposure to fossil fuels" (Mooney 2017).

In short, several factors are conspiring to raise expectations regarding the conduct of investment governance by fiduciaries.

The Response from Fiduciaries

As asset owners grow larger, and because they are being held to the higher standards, the need for effective investment governance processes and practices increases. This idea is widely accepted by fiduciary bodies, but the responses from asset owners have been mixed.

We categorize the responses from what we define as least desirable to most desirable as follows:

- *Negative*—The negative response has a narrow focus on legal compliance. Such a fiduciary is most interested in keeping off the radar of the regulator—and out of court.[10] Although all approaches should pursue

---

[8]Debate about the Fiduciary Rule is ongoing. The rule was proposed and promulgated by the Obama administration but has not been fully implemented. On 29 June 2017, the Department of Labor released a request for public comments—the fifth such request—on its new "investment advice" fiduciary definition and related exemptions.

[9]Employee Retirement Income Security Act; Fiduciary Rule, 81 Fed. Reg. 20946 (8 April 2016) (to be codified at 29 C.F.R. pts. 2509, 2510, and 2550).

[10]See Aikin (2017) for a high-level discussion.

these legal goals, the negative approach is principally concerned with what is in the *fiduciary's* best interests, namely, management of the fiduciary's career risk. According to this view, the best interests of the beneficiary will be served by the fiduciary complying with the letter of the law. When the law codifies a standard that provides only a minimum of protections, the beneficiary misses out on the higher standards we advocate in this study.

- *Positive*—A positive response occurs when the institution's governing body takes a more *strategic approach* to investment governance—that is, using it to improve decision making and facilitate risk management with a view toward adding value for beneficiaries and other stakeholders. Such a response sees investment governance as a means of ensuring compliance (as one element of risk management) *and* as a driver of excellence and continuous improvement.

- *Best-practice stewardship*—What we argue is the ideal response is one that satisfies the prior two categories but is guided by a sincere commitment to act in the interests of the beneficiary. The principal weakness with the positive response is that, although it does *seek* to add value and drive excellence, these benefits may not necessarily accrue to the beneficiary. Instead, the benefits might accrue to management (and/or their agents) at the expense of the beneficiaries. For instance, at a pension plan, the short-term interests of management may be served by adopting a certain investment strategy but one that does not benefit long-term performance. For example, the plan may seek to better its peer-relative performance, for which management earns short-term incentives, at the expense of the long-term interests of beneficiaries. Although such behavior is suboptimal for beneficiaries, it could be seen as excellent by some standards. In contrast, best-practice stewardship is defined as putting the interests of the beneficiary (the principal) central in such a way that orients investment governance structure and mechanims to this purpose (refer **Exhibit 1**).

This study identifies and discusses the essential components of an investment governance framework that allows fiduciaries to fulfill their duties diligently and effectively (e.g., see the OECD framework in **Exhibit 1**).

A Framework

Having defined and discussed the *why* of investment governance, we turn to the question of *how* to bring it to bear as an essential component of good fiduciary practice. In this chapter, we provide only a basic outline of the

Exhibit 1. OECD Guidelines for Pension Fund Governance

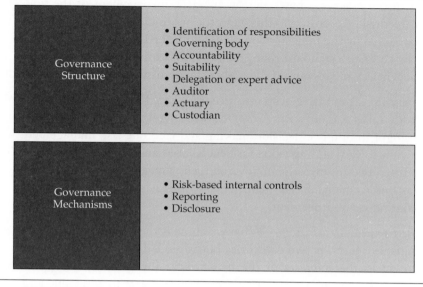

Governance Structure
- Identification of responsibilities
- Governing body
- Accountability
- Suitability
- Delegation or expert advice
- Auditor
- Actuary
- Custodian

Governance Mechanisms
- Risk-based internal controls
- Reporting
- Disclosure

Source: OECD (2009).

framework and give a small number of practical examples. The balance of the book elaborates on this framework.

The framework we are introducing is not, in and of itself, fully original. We have worked in institutional investing for many years and have come across various versions of this framework and the process that is central to it.[11] Over time, the framework has been added to and edited such that it appears in its current form (see the *OPERIS* framework in **Exhibit 2**).

At this point, the reader might expect investment professionals to launch into a discussion about an investment process focused on the *best* way to capture returns. We take a different view. Achieving outcomes on behalf of beneficiaries is as much about *managing risks* as it is about *capturing returns*—and we mean "risks" broadly construed, not simply fluctuations in asset values.

Our preferred metaphor for this investment process emphasizes the *defensive* aspects of solving the investment challenge, especially defending the beneficiary from risk events and/or uncompensated risks (as well as capturing returns). Given the uncertainty around investment decision making, the

---

[11]In particular, we would like to acknowledge the following organizations and their past and present staff: the Myer Family Company, QSuper, QIC, Willis Towers Watson (and its former manifestations), and Equipsuper. Through our work at and with these organizations, and through our work with individuals who have worked at these organizations, we have developed and improved this process.

Exhibit 2. The *OPERIS* Investment Governance Framework

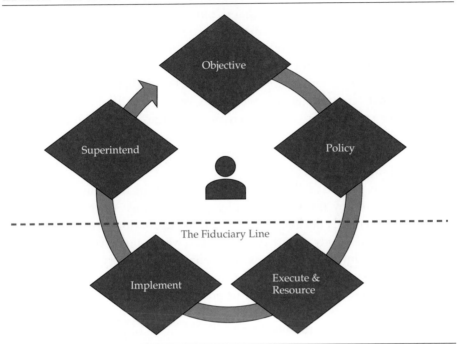

fiduciary investor—that is, the body or person managing the assets of another group of people—is left to rely on a robust process.

To underscore the idea of defense, we have adopted a Latin word used to describe field defenses, *operis*, as the way to remember the key steps of our investment process.[12] Exhibit 2 shows the outline of the investment governance framework, which calls to mind the shape of a medieval form of fortification known as a bastion fort, or *trace italienne*.

We cover this process in detail in subsequent chapters, but at this point, note that the first letters of the key steps spell out the defensive approach of *OPERIS*: **O**bjective, **P**olicy, **E**xecute and **R**esource, **I**mplement, **S**uperintend.

First, by "defensive" we do not mean what a professional investor might think of as being defensive (i.e., holding a large weight in bonds or low-risk

---

[12]Our reference in this regard is a passage out of *The Gallic Wars* by Julius Caesar (Book 1, Chapter 8), as follows: "The Helvetii, disappointed in this hope, tried if they could force a passage (some by means of a bridge of boats and numerous rafts constructed for the purpose; others, by the fords of the Rhone, where the depth of the river was least, sometimes by day, but more frequently by night), but being kept at bay by the strength of our works [*operis mūnitiōne*, in the original Latin], and by the concourse of the soldiers, and by the missiles, they desisted from this attempt" (emphasis added).

stocks), we mean the fiduciary *defending* the beneficiary, to the greatest extent possible, from the misadventures that the investment industry can offer.

Second, the process is continuous. It is not simply considered and approved by the governing body, put in place, and then consigned to the filing cabinet to reappear only when the regulator asks to see it. Implemented as intended, *OPERIS* is an *ongoing* process (of defense) that is repeatedly revisited to facilitate continuous improvement. Consistent with a commitment to best-practice stewardship, our concern is to do the best by the beneficiary. The fiduciary achieves this goal not only by making effective strategic decisions but also by having a defensible, repeatable, and documented process as evidence of due diligence.

Third, the process is designed to be universal, in that any investor can apply it to solve any investment challenge. The process does not provide a universal answer. It is flexible; it is only a framework. Some readers may find this aspect of the study unsatisfying because we do not give an *n*-step formula for certain investment success. We believe our industry may contain too much of this type of "silver-bullet" thinking. Some people seem to believe that there exists some *magic strategy* or product that greatly simplifies investing or assures success. This misperception is probably a function of the business realities of modern financial firms. The promise or perception of a silver bullet may allow investment firms to spend more time, in Ellis's terms, on "the economics of the business"—that is, attempting to drive investment firm profitability through the sale of highly scalable products—than on "the values of the profession"—pursuing the idiosyncratic, and notoriously difficult to achieve, investment objectives of real, human clients (Ellis 2011).[13]

Fourth, the "fiduciary line" shown in Exhibit 2 is of great importance because it separates the key strategic governance steps above the line from the implementation functions that take place below the line. The fiduciary line has important implications for investment governance that will be explored throughout this study.

The fiduciary line also reveals one of the great challenges to effective investment governance. As mentioned previously, the interests of asset consultants can diverge from those of the fiduciaries they are advising if they are providing advice on matters of both investment policy (above the fiduciary line) and investment selection (below the line). The conflict arises when the consultant earns more money below the fiduciary line (which we would argue they do) but use their influence among fiduciaries to advocate decisions above the fiduciary line that benefit them.

---

[13]Ellis has always brought to the debate a nice balance between academic rigor and practitioner pragmatism. See, for example, Ellis (2013, 2016) and Malkiel and Ellis (2013).

A classic example is the question of whether to implement the investment policy portfolio by using active managers or by using index funds. If the consultant earns significant fees from manager selection services, they have an incentive to advocate for active management as an investment belief, or deemphasize the case for passive management. In such a case, the consultant might be tempted to prioritize "the economics of the business" (i.e., earning fees from manager selection) over the "the values of the profession" (i.e., ensuring portfolio positions are appropriate for the fiduciaries acting on behalf of beneficiaries) (Ellis 2011).

Finally, this process does not exist in a vacuum. Every process takes place in an organizational context, and investment governance is no different. The context must be considered.

Contextual Issues

Several key contextual issues may affect the way in which the investment governance process is implemented.

Nature of the Investment Challenge. Not all investment issues are the same, so the best way to implement the process will vary accordingly. On one hand, for a DC plan with thousands, or even hundreds of thousands, of plan members ranging in age from early 20s to mid-60s, with diverse careers, simplifying the plan's investment objectives is difficult. Some plan members will be focused on accumulating wealth; others will be more focused on protecting the wealth it has taken a working life to build. Thus, the DC plan may seek to segment its membership by age, occupation, or another meaningful attribute. Such an approach will likely result in several investment portfolios—target risk, target date, or some other design—each pursuing differently framed objectives. On the other hand, the investment issue may be relatively simple for a charitable trust. In many jurisdictions, such trusts have a minimum spending rate (e.g., 5% of the corpus), which leads neatly into a headline investment objective: inflation plus 5% per year. The headline objective might be neat, but the likelihood of achieving it in current market conditions is another issue.

Organizational Context. A range of professionals assists fiduciaries in addressing the investment task they face.[14] These professionals may be

---

[14]See the ongoing research program on pension fund capitalism by Gordon L. Clark, University of Oxford (Clark 1993, 2000, 2003, 2012, 2017). We commend Clark's latest research collaboration with Ashby Monk, Stanford University, on institutional investors in global markets (Clark and Monk 2017). We also recommend the work of Keith P. Ambachtsheer, who has written extensively on pension fund governance and management over many years (see Ambachtsheer and Ezra 1998; Ambachtsheer 2007, 2016).

employees of the organization for which the fiduciaries fulfill their governance role, or they may belong to one of several service providers (e.g., asset consultants, actuaries). The resources used by fiduciaries in fulfilling their investment obligations according to the preceding investment process are a function of such factors as scale, complexity, and nature of the investment problem.

The simplest structure might entail the board of trustees of, say, a small school foundation, which outsources the investment problem to one or more qualified outsourced chief investment officers—for example, an "implemented" consultant. At the other end of the spectrum, the complexity of investment arrangements is virtually unlimited. We have been involved with organizations that have significant internal teams that are supplemented by a panel of asset consultants and a large number of investment managers and general partner relationships.

The nature of the particular organization may also influence the way the investment task is managed on an ongoing basis. For example, a pension fund might see the investment function as very much part of its core value proposition—and for this reason it is not surprising that the investment process of the largest pension funds in many countries is substantially internalized. In contrast, some corporations with pension obligations may prefer to outsource the investment function because pension investing is not viewed as part of that corporation's core business. This form has become common in the United States.

Governance Budget. The nature of the investment challenge and the organizational context influence (or ought to influence) what has become known as "the governance budget" (Clark and Urwin 2008). The governance budget is the "finite and conceptually measurable resource" (such as "time, talent, and treasure") allocated to "create value from effective actions in the chain of institution-defined tasks and functions" (Clark and Urwin, pp. 4–5; see also Watson Wyatt 2004). We return to this idea of a metaphorical chain of trusted relationships in Chapters 6 and 7. The size of the governance budget ought to be consistent with the nature of the task at hand. A simple investment task, therefore, should require a modest governance budget; a highly complex investment challenge, a significant one.

Who Decides What? Who Does What? Investment governance is essentially about effective investment decision making in pursuit of some set of investment objectives designed to address a given investment challenge. Related questions include who, or what body, makes which investment decisions and to whom are certain investment functions delegated? These questions are especially relevant for large and/or complex investment challenges for which significant governance and management resources must typically be dedicated. For example, at a large DC pension plan, a governing body (e.g., a board of trustees), an investment committee consisting of a subset of the board,[15] a chief executive officer, a chief investment officer, one or more asset consultants, an internal investment team, and many external investment managers—all are likely. Considering the multiple roles and array of resources, who decides what and who does what?

In answering these questions, we emphasize that, no matter how the roles are assigned and the responsibilities delegated, the accountability remains with the governing body. For this reason, roles and responsibilities must be understood by all parties and be documented in a statement (or matrix) of delegations. We return to the issues about clarity of roles and responsibilities in Chapter 8 when we consider the *"OPERIS stack."*

In their own words ...

"Investment governance is critical to long-term investment success. It allows the board and investment committee to set very clear objectives and priorities, while explicitly grappling with risk trade-offs, and to clearly articulate the 'rules of play.' Thereby, good investment governance empowers management to exercise its delegations with confidence, knowing that it is making decisions which are fully aligned with what the board and investment committee are seeking."

—*Sonya Sawtell-Rickson, Chief Investment Officer, HESTA*

Use of Metaphors

Throughout this book, we use metaphors that, we hope, bring to life the ideas we discuss, namely, flying and driving. The flying/airplane metaphor, having been suggested by Blake, Cairns, and Dowd (2009) as appropriate for illustrating DC plans, is relatively common in pension finance. Furthermore, the "glidepath" referred to in the design of target-date funds is suggestive of a successful flight achieved by negotiating the descent and safe landing of the aircraft.

The Nobel Laureate Robert Merton preferred the automobile metaphor. He considered the automobile to be the metaphorical vehicle that gets one to

---

[15]See the excellent work of Bailey and Richards (2017) on understanding investment committee responsibilities.

the desired destination—that is, "an appropriate standard of living in retirement" (Merton 2007).[16] Merton's key point was that you do not have to know how to build a car to drive a car; investment strategies designed for the individual, in his view, should have the same characteristic—easy to use although possibly concealing sophisticated design under the hood.

The point is that this investment governance framework, and the associated investment process, is designed to achieve an investment objective—that is, *get to a particular destination* (by metaphorical plane or car). Properly defining and communicating the investment objective (i.e., the destination) is the necessary first step in effective investment governance. As noted, we look at the nature of the investment objective from three perspectives: a DC plan, a DB plan, and an endowment or foundation.

The car and plane metaphors are rich in meaning. Take, for example, the plane analogy. The destination (investment success) is usually some distance (time) away (in the future). To reach the destination, the investor must

- select an appropriate aircraft (investment strategy) for the task,

- appoint a qualified and capable crew (investment organization),

- chart the journey (set the investment policy),

- operate the plane (manage the portfolios), and

- respond to prevailing flying conditions, which can be difficult and change suddenly (adjust the portfolio for changes in markets or in the investment objective).

We are talking about inputs *into* the process and outputs *from* the process. This *dual focus* is a theme of this study.

These metaphors clearly, however, have limitations.[17] For example, buying a plane ticket almost always results in the traveler reaching her or his destination even if for some reason arrival is delayed. The same cannot be said of investment objectives. The probability of achieving reasonable investment objectives is lower (actually, much lower) than the probability of arriving

---

[16]Note that Merton's essential point is less about the investment objective—although that does feature—than about the design of the automobile (i.e., plan design). Merton used the metaphor to discuss the ride more than the destination. He argued that, given the complexity of the retirement planning challenge and the limited skills and motivations most individuals have to solve it, those who design DC plans must make "driving" to the destination as simple as possible.

[17]Yet, Blake et al. (2009) contended, and we agree, that even the deficiencies of the metaphor are "highly instructive" (p. 39).

for your Hawaiian vacation. We will acknowledge when the metaphor is stretched.

A Final Word

As mentioned earlier in the chapter, an important distinction must be made between *investment governance* expertise and *investment* expertise. This study focuses primarily on the former, though it does touch on the latter. One need not have a Ph.D. in finance to be an effective investment fiduciary. Being a fiduciary who is competent in matters of investment governance is more about good *process* than it is about technical knowledge in finance, in the same way that being a nonexecutive director of General Motors does not require one to be an automotive engineer or mechanic. Nevertheless, investment governance does require the "effective use of resources" (i.e., people, policies, processes, and systems) to solve the underlying investment issue, including engaging and overseeing the work of investment experts.

Points for Reflection: Chapter 1. Why Investment Governance?

As a fiduciary:

- Can I succinctly summarize the underlying investment challenge?

- Do I know who my principals (or beneficiaries) are? Do I understand what they might expect of me as a fiduciary?

- Have I thought about how agency risk might apply to my situation?

- Am I comfortable with my level of capability in light of the complexity of the investment portfolios I govern?

- Am I aware of the expectations of stakeholders (defined broadly) regarding my role as a fiduciary?

- Do I fit the definition of a best-practice steward?

- Am I involved in a continuous investment process (i.e., one that is periodically revisited and revised)?

- Do I have a complete understanding of the context—economic, strategic, and so forth—in which the organization exists?

- Can I succinctly summarize what investment success for my beneficiaries looks like?

2. Investment Beliefs: Decision Making in Context

"To believe in something, and *not to live it*, is dishonest."

—*Mahatma (Mohandas K.) Gandhi*[18]

Before we embark on a more detailed exploration of the *OPERIS* investment governance framework, we return briefly to the investment process introduced in Chapter 1.

In this chapter and Chapter 3, we focus exclusively on the first step in the process, defining the **O**bjective (Step O), as highlighted in **Exhibit 3**. This step is the most important one for fiduciaries because it results, if done properly, in as complete an understanding of the underlying investment issue as can be achieved. By properly defining and documenting the investment challenge, the governing body, to use our metaphors, correctly identifies the journey's *destination* (i.e., the investment objective or objectives) and the preferred *way to make the journey* (i.e., the investment strategy). If the destination is incorrectly identified, then a fiduciary is prone to use an ill-suited vehicle (automobile or aircraft), or give incorrect instructions to the driver/pilot and crew (who operate mostly below the fiduciary line). If the preferred type of journey is not understood (the investment strategy), the ride may be such that reaching the destination will be difficult or impossible (because of, say, capitulation risk[19]).

Furthermore, because of the fiduciary's duty to, and relationship with, the beneficiary, the fiduciary is the party best placed to—and in some cases, the only party able to—understand the details and nuances of the investment problem to be solved. Investment managers, who are employed below the fiduciary line, often cannot directly observe the needs or behavior of the beneficiaries, nor do they necessarily know the headline investment objectives of the overall investment program. Instead, they are hired to fulfill a defined mandate that, in turn, has its place in the investment policy approved by the governing body and implemented via (internal and/or external) management.

---

[18]Mohandas K. Gandhi was an Indian lawyer, politician, social activist, and writer who became the leader of the Indian independence movement.

[19]Capitulation risk is the term used "to describe the risk that investors will abandon equities at the worst possible time" (Drew and Walk 2016, p. 28). From the perspective of our metaphors, an overly aggressive investment strategy (a rough ride) might result in capitulation risk, thus jeopardizing the beneficiary's chances of achieving the objective (reaching the destination). To our knowledge, the term "capitulation risk" was first coined by Simon Kitson of QDRA.

Exhibit 3. *OPERIS* **Framework: Objective, Part 1**

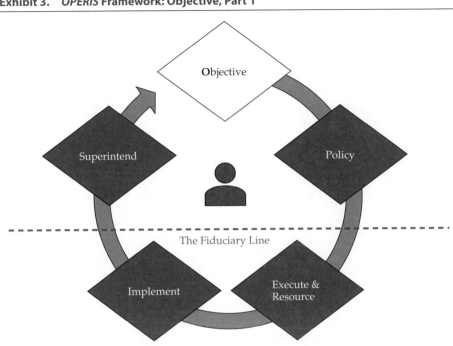

The setting of objectives also drives (or should drive!) all subsequent decisions, and any actual or potential investment decision can and should be evaluated in light of the objective. Thus, Step O establishes the necessary context for all subsequent decisions that management makes to implement the investment policy arrived at by fiduciaries on behalf of beneficiaries.

These principles may seem obvious, but we devote two chapters to setting objectives because, first, this primary step is the critical step for fiduciaries. It is the task for which they bear the greatest responsibility and to which they can add the greatest value because of their knowledge of the beneficiary. Therefore, to act in the interests of the beneficiaries, fiduciaries ought to know the interests of the beneficiary well, and act in those interests (and not in their own). Second, we focus on this first step because *much of the investment industry is not the slightest bit interested in it.*

Investment managers are generally interested in their own process and the extent to which it results in product sales. According to this view of the world, one dollar of assets under management (AUM) is as good as another as long as the dollar generates the same level of fees. Put another way, to secure the marginal dollar of AUM, investment managers are incentivized to convince fiduciaries, and the executives who act on behalf of fiduciaries, that their product is helpful to fiduciaries in solving their investment problem, whether or not the manager knows what it is.

We would argue that some investment managers do not have a great basis on which to make the claim that their product will be useful. Moreover, a number of the incentives confronting investment managers militate against their acting in the interests of beneficiaries, who are, more or less, unknown to them. For example, managers and beneficiaries have opposing interests in relation to management fees. That investment products have a role to play is undisputed; that all of them are equally beneficial is obviously untrue. Investment beliefs, and properly framed investment objectives, can help fiduciaries sift through the universe of investment opportunities by evaluating each opportunity for its alignment with the beneficiary's interests.

Investment Beliefs

We define investment beliefs as the governing body's set of guiding principles for investing. Some might prefer to call these principles a "philosophy" or something less emotionally loaded than beliefs, but whatever the preferred term, we consider *having* investment beliefs and *holding true* to an investment philosophy as synonymous and treat them as such in this chapter.

The risk when talking about investment beliefs is that the conversation can become an exercise in *abstract* generalities. To make the discussion concrete, we begin by outlining a set of beliefs. We are not trying to convince the reader of the truth of these beliefs; we are simply outlining a set of beliefs to highlight how one might go about expressing them. The form and expression of the following beliefs are thus more important for the reader than their content.

This working set of investment beliefs is as follows:

1. *Rigorous simplicity is best.* Given the nature of the financial sector, unnecessary complexity is easy to create. When considering initiatives, we carefully consider whether any additional complexity is outweighed by expected benefits.

2. *Markets are dynamic.* Not only are financial markets dynamic, so too are the interrelationships between markets. They are subject to rapid and unpredictable change. We design, invest, and monitor investment portfolios with this dynamism in mind.

3. *Asset pricing anomalies abound.* Research shows that financial markets exhibit multiple asset pricing anomalies. To efficiently and effectively capture returns, we design, invest, and monitor investment portfolios with these anomalies in mind.

4. *The error term is large.* Acknowledging the limitations of the state of the art and the scientific methods used in the industry, we admit that the probability of being incorrect is significant. We attempt to invest in a way that is robust to error.

5. *End-investor objectives are paramount.* Investing should be conducted with a view toward helping beneficiaries achieve their goals (meet the investment challenge). All other considerations are subordinated to this goal.

6. *Asset allocation is the central focus.* Research shows that the asset allocation decision is a key driver of portfolio returns. It accounts for a significant portion of the differences between outcomes of different portfolios (Brinson, Hood, and Beebower 1986; Ibbotson and Kaplan 2000; Statman 2001; Scott, Balsamo, McShane, and Tasopoulos 2017). Therefore, fiduciaries should spend a significant amount of time agreeing on an asset allocation policy with the highest probability of achieving investment objectives and proportionally less time on subordinate (but perhaps more interesting) decisions (e.g., manager selection). Implicit in this belief is a further belief: a diversified portfolio of market returns—or beta exposures, in the vernacular—does most of the heavy lifting when it comes to achieving investment objectives.

7. *Timeframes matter.* For pension finance applications, the investment time horizon is a critical variable.[20] When designing portfolios—particularly those that are not perpetual in nature—the different investment horizons of beneficiaries must be considered.

---

[20]Much of finance theory assumes that a given return—say, 10%—is of equal significance whether it is earned in the first or the last year of a period over which an investment is held. This equality is true only if no cash flows in or out of the portfolio (no contributions or withdrawals are made). Obviously, when considering a person saving for retirement or spending down assets in retirement, this assumption is completely wrong. Only in the special case of no contributions or withdrawals are time-weighted returns the appropriate lens through which to evaluate performance. In a pension finance context—in which wealth is a function of returns and contributions and withdrawals and compounding effects—the timing of a return is critical. To illustrate the point, consider this: If you earned a –10% return, would you prefer it to be in Year 1 of your working life (on an account balance of, say, $5,000) or in Year 39 of your working life (on an account balance of, say, $500,000)? Obviously, the latter loss of 10% is far more destructive because a loss applies to all previous years' compounded wealth and contributions. In this context, money-weighted or dollar-weighted returns are the appropriate lens through which to evaluate performance. The portfolio size effect (the dynamics of wealth accumulation) and sequencing risk (the risk of receiving a disadvantageous sequence of returns rather than the mean of the return path) underline the importance of an investment horizon in practical investing (Basu and Drew 2009; Milevsky and Macqueen 2010; Basu, Byrne, and Drew 2011; Bianchi, Drew, Evans, and Walk 2014; Bianchi, Drew, and Walk 2014, 2016 [a]). In Chapter 9, we advocate a dual focus when evaluating performance.

8. *Risk must be defined and managed.* Traditional finance theory and practice tend to define risk as the standard deviation of arithmetic (time-weighted) returns. Behavioral research has revealed that real humans—as opposed to the (fictitious) rational *homo economicus*—experience risk differently, with measures like drawdown being more representative of actual risk attitudes than, say, standard deviation. Furthermore, research shows that risk preferences are a more sophisticated concept than simply risk tolerance.[21] Therefore, we define risk in ways meaningful for both fiduciaries and their beneficiaries and then manage portfolios in light of these settings.

9. *Active skill is rare but valuable.* The debate regarding the benefits or detriments of active management is extensive and ongoing. We believe that generating excess returns after fees and taxes is a challenging proposition and that identifying such active skill *ex ante* is equally challenging. Therefore, we target markets and strategies for which prospective active opportunities are likely to be most attractive (i.e., where a skill premium is most likely to exist) within an agreed fee budget.

10. *Effective implementation adds value.* Implementation takes the approved investment policy and brings it to life. Efficient and effective implementation (e.g., hedging, tax management, liquidity management) can add value through incremental return, avoided costs, and/or improved risk management.

We recommend that the following aspects be considered by fiduciaries when resolving and documenting investment beliefs:

- *Clear statement*—Briefly state the belief in such a way that it can be comprehended by all stakeholders.

- *Implications*—Preempt the question "so what?" That is, rather than leaving the reader of the beliefs to imagine what a belief might mean in terms of tangible action, spell out the implications explicitly.

- *Evidence*—To demonstrate that the beliefs "are lived"—as our opening quote from Gandhi exhorts us to do—evidence of the belief in action would be beneficial. Fiduciaries might ask the question, "Is this initiative consistent with our investment beliefs?" as a way of holding management accountable to the agreed investment beliefs. If management doesn't have a satisfactory answer to this question, perhaps the management is not integrating investment beliefs into the investment process.

---

[21]We discuss risk preferences in detail in Chapter 3.

- *References*—Being academics as well as practitioners, we cannot resist the temptation to recommend citing academic and/or practitioner research to validate beliefs. Having such support is not necessarily proof positive that a belief is well founded, but it does demonstrate that the fiduciary has researched the belief and found scientific evidence that the belief is reasonable. Having a belief that has no academic evidence to support it is something we would not recommend without significant further research and consideration.

Exhibit 4 provides an example of how to document an investment belief.

To advocate for the resolution and documentation of investment beliefs, one must see in them a purpose or set of benefits. We contend that the

Exhibit 4. Important Elements of Investment Beliefs/Principles: Element Example

Element	Example
Clear Statement	• Asset allocation is the central focus — Research shows that the asset allocation decision drives portfolio returns, accounting for 80% or more of the differences between outcomes of different portfolios
Implications	• Fiduciaries should spend a significant amount of time agreeing on an investment policy with the highest probability of achieving investment objectives • Fiduciaries should spend proportionally less on subordinate (but perhaps more interesting) decisions (e.g., manager selection) • A diversified portfolio of market returns — or beta, in the vernacular — does most of the heavy lifting when it comes to achieving investment objectives
Evidence (in practice)	• Asset allocation is a permanent agenda item on the agendas of all board and management boards/committees • Minutes record significant discussions regarding asset allocation • Manager and investment selection is less of a priority for the board and/or is delegated to management • Fees and costs are spent on asset allocation more than on other activities
References	• Brinson, Hood, and Beebower (1986) • Ibbotson and Kaplan (2000) • Statman (2001) • Scott, Balsamo, McShane, and Tasopoulos (2017)

following are main reasons for having an agreed and documented set of investment beliefs:

- They clarify and summarize the essential investment philosophy of the governing body.

- As Lydenberg (2011) noted, investment beliefs act as "a bridge between high-level goals and practical decision making." Thus, beliefs may be used as criteria for evaluating marginal investment decisions and prioritizing initiatives, ensuring alignment between philosophical outlook and action.

- They provide a single set of truths to be held (at least for the purposes of investing at the particular entity), thus superseding the personal views of individuals involved in the investment ecosystem.[22]

- When market conditions are volatile, investment beliefs can be used to stiffen—or, given the *OPERIS* framework, fortify—resolve by providing a set of well-thought-through and closely held truths.

In their own words ...

"By being clear about investment beliefs, delegations, and account-abilities the investment organization—boards, investment committees and investment professionals—can focus on creating outcomes for end beneficiaries."

—Danielle Press, Commissioner, Australian Securities and Investments Commission

Types of Investment Beliefs

Investment beliefs generally fall into one of two categories:

- *Positive beliefs*—Many investment beliefs—for example, the belief outlined previously relating to asset allocation—emerge from the positive insights of peer-reviewed scientific (or social scientific) research. Put simply, positive beliefs represent *the way the world is.*

---

[22]A hallmark of professionalism is that the investment staff serving a governing body subordinate their personal investment beliefs to those of the organization for which they work. If a member of the investment staff finds he or she cannot act according to the organization's beliefs, that staff person should resign.

- *Normative beliefs*—Other investment beliefs focus more on the fiduciary's vision for the world. For example, when the empirical evidence regarding environmental, social, and governance (ESG) factors in investing is mixed, some fiduciaries pursue such an approach on normative grounds.[23] That is, fiduciaries form the view that investing by considering ESG factors is consistent with their fiduciary duty to beneficiaries and indicative of good stewardship. By defining beneficiaries in this context, fiduciaries tend to take an expansive view of their duties by including other stakeholders (e.g., the community) within their definition of what is meant by a beneficiary. Normative beliefs represent *the way the world ought to be.*

For investment governance, not only will the fiduciary benefit from being aware of the nature of the investment belief, but it is also important to ensure that the type of investment belief is consistent with the role the fiduciary plays in the investment ecosystem. By this we mean that the investment belief ought to be *relevant* in light of the nature of a fiduciary's role.

As discussed, in a large pension fund, numerous parties are involved in fulfilling the investment function, including the following:

- *Ultimate governing body*—Because of its legal duty to beneficiaries, this body must represent the beneficiary's best interests.

- *Investment committee*—Due to the complexity of investment arrangements, key investment accountabilities are sometimes delegated to a committee of the governing body so that greater scrutiny can be applied to important investment questions. Increasingly, we see investment committees consisting of highly expert members, including those who are otherwise independent from the investment organization.

- *Management*—Internal management, including the chief investment officer and their staff, also may be delegated certain tasks (e.g., those tasks that require more frequent attention than the governing body or the investment committee is able to devote to the task because of a limited governance budget).

---

[23]Some fiduciaries have been reluctant to incorporate ESG factors in their investing approach because the empirical evidence about its added value is not convincing. These fiduciaries take their (common law) fiduciary duty to beneficiaries to mean maximizing financial return. From this perspective, the thought is that fiduciaries expose themselves to legal liability by pursuing an investment belief for which the evidence is mixed at best. We will discuss ESG factors in investing in detail in the next section.

- *Asset consultant(s)*—At large pension funds, one or more consultants may be used to assist with tasks related to the investment challenge (e.g., actuarial modeling, manager selection).

- *Investment manager(s)*—Complex pension plans typically have numerous investment managers appointed across the full range of asset classes and investment strategies. Each of these investment managers (internal or external) is evaluated before being appointed to fulfill a particular role in the plan, according to a documented mandate.

Clearly, each of these parties could have his or her own investment beliefs (although those of the governing body and the investment committee should be the same). The point is that each party's investment beliefs should be relevant *to each one's role*. For example, it is entirely reasonable—we would say desirable—for a governing body to have one or more investment beliefs that focus on the beneficiary. After all, the beneficiary should be the prime object of the fiduciary's attention. We would be much more surprised for a governing body's investment beliefs to include a highly technical opinion about a particular asset class (e.g., that backwardation is a feature of the markets for commodity futures that makes it a desirable investment proposition). Such a belief may be supported by evidence, but how might this belief be acted upon by the governing body (as opposed to one of its delegates)? Investment beliefs should be consistent with the remit of the party that holds the beliefs.

Conversely, an active investment manager in US equities should quite rightly have investment beliefs that relate to the manager's ability to earn a skill premium from a preferred opportunity set (e.g., small-capitalization stocks). For such a manager to have explicit views about how to serve beneficiaries would be unusual—beyond the truth that any active return earned, after fees and taxes (and after adjustment for any risk taken beyond that of the benchmark), assists fiduciaries in achieving their investment objectives on behalf of beneficiaries. The role of the asset managers is to act in their client's best interests by fulfilling the mandate for which they have been appointed—for example, by beating an appropriately chosen benchmark for that particular mandate.

ESG Issues

The investment industry has seen increased interest in a type of investing that is known variously as ethical investing, socially responsible investing, sustainable investing, or investing by considering ESG factors.[24] The ESG label is

---

[24]See the work of Woods and Urwin (2010) on frameworks that fiduciary investors can consider for the implementation of a sustainable investing strategy.

currently the preferred one, because the others, such as ethical investing, are thought to be overly normative. (In this context, by *normative*, we mean advocating a defined set of ESG beliefs that may or may not be universally held.) From personal experience at a large pension plan, we argue that it is impossible to identify ESG factors that are universally accepted by plan members. For some memberships—for example, ones built around a religion or institutions associated with a religion (such as Catholic schools)—some sort of consensus on priority ESG factors, if not on all such factors, may be possible.

ESG investing is discussed here because it is an increasingly common investment belief among investment fiduciaries, and it raises complex issues. Fiduciaries usually take the view that it is incumbent on them, as the stewards of significant wealth on behalf of members of the community, to maximize risk-adjusted return but also to do so in a way that avoids harm and/or promotes good. Such a view leads to two questions:

- What does the fiduciary define as *harmful* and *good*?

- How does the fiduciary avoid harm (however defined) and promote good (however defined)?

As the ESG label suggests, the definitions of harmful and good may be divided into three broad categories: environmental, social, and governance factors. Within these categories there are relatively obvious criteria. On one hand, given the present focus on the use of fossil fuels, so-called *carbon intensity* is a reasonably predictable environmental criterion by which to judge an investment proposition. Respect for indigenous rights, on the other hand, is a social criterion that might not immediately spring to the mind of every fiduciary. When ESG factors figure in the investment beliefs of the governing body, an important role of fiduciaries, together with their advisers, is to determine the set of ESG criteria that properly represents the views of plan membership.[25]

To give the reader a sense of the possible range of approaches, we provide the following examples:

- Sustainalytics, a global leader in ESG and corporate governance research, uses 145 ESG indicators to evaluate companies. The STOXX ESG Leaders Index—a global index published by STOXX based on Sustainalytics research—identifies the "best performing" companies

---

[25]An approach we have observed is for fiduciaries to establish an ESG investment option that plan members may select as an alternative to applying ESG criteria to all plan investment options. Even in this case, fiduciaries need to define the ESG criteria for such an option, and not all plan members may be satisfied with the ESG criteria.

based on 134 "financially material" ESG indicators. In addition to using these criteria to identify the best performers, STOXX automatically excludes companies if they are involved in "controversial weapons" (e.g., antipersonnel mines and cluster munitions) and/or are identified as the "worst offenders" according to United Nations norms.

- One way to look at activities that cause *harm*, and might be considered in defining the fiduciary's ESG criteria, is to consider a "unique" investment process. The Vice Fund "is designed for investors seeking to capture better long-term risk-adjusted returns than the S&P 500 Index by investing in stocks within industries that demonstrate significant barriers to entry, including tobacco, alcoholic beverages, gaming and defense/aerospace industries" (USA Mutuals 2017). Note that the purported rationale for the investment strategy is "barriers to entry," but the fund is unashamedly named "The Vice Fund." The suggestion is that the "vice" aspects of these investments are at least acknowledged by the distributors of the fund. The rationale for the investment opportunity is that ESG investors, by avoiding these stocks, make the prices more attractive to non-ESG investors. It suffices to say that these are some of the exposures that would be excluded by fiduciaries that take a strict view in relation to ESG criteria.[26]

The reader may have noticed that a question embedded in these two examples is *how* these ESG criteria are reflected in portfolios under the governing body's stewardship. To carry out the ESG strategy, the fiduciary must decide whether to use a negative or a positive screen:

- *Negative screen*—The classical approach to ESG investing is to *screen out* those companies or investments that are inconsistent with the fiduciary's ESG criteria. For example, like the STOXX ESG Leaders Index, the screen might exclude controversial weapons and perhaps other activities that may be viewed as undesirable (e.g., uranium mining). As suggested in Chapter 1, a popular negative screen seeks to exclude those companies involved in the production of fossil fuels. Social activists might negatively screen out those companies that have poor worker rights records or that have been shown to use child labor in their supply chains. Religious investors might exclude companies that are involved in activities inconsistent with their own moral teachings (e.g., pornography, contraception, abortifacients).

- *Positive screen*—Instead of punishing activities inconsistent with a plan's ESG criteria, one approach is to reward positive activities. For example,

---

[26]For further discussion on this sort of investment strategy, see Richey (2016).

a company that commits to using renewable energy might attract the interest of those investors that positively screen the opportunity set for responsible environmental decision making.

Although these approaches seem simple enough, several complicating questions need to be addressed before an investment portfolio can reflect ESG principles. For example, negative screening, by its nature, means that "ethical" investors cease to have any involvement with companies that are involved in activities the fiduciary judges to be undesirable. So, the share registry of these companies is left to those investors with fewer scruples or different standards. If the objective of ESG investing is to improve corporate behavior, abstaining from investing in a company is unlikely to work well.

Positive screening seeks to reward positive ESG performance. Positive behavior may exist, however, in industries or companies that might also be excluded via negative screens. For example, take a mining company that has some exposure to fossil fuels but has industry-leading corporate governance and environmental reporting practices. Should such a company be excluded because of the fossil fuel exposure alone or retained because of its admirable approach to corporate governance? Ultimately, not all ESG decisions are clear-cut; they often involve uncomfortable judgment calls.

Also, in practice, practical questions exist about the materiality of a company's exposure to the desirable or undesirable activity. A pure approach would see a company screened out (excluded) if it had any exposure to a negative ESG factor. Thus, a company with minor exposure would be dealt with in the same way as a company whose only line of business is the undesirable activity.

A more pragmatic approach to, say, negative screening would exclude a company only if the exposure to the undesirable activity is beyond a certain threshold (e.g., the company earns greater than 20% of total income from the activity). Such an approach is practical, but it does leave the fiduciary open to the critique that, after all, things are not just 20% undesirable; they either are desirable or not.

In introducing this section, we said that fiduciaries usually regard it as their obligation to invest in a way that avoids harm and/or promotes good. This concern has not always been considered. Earlier in our careers, we often heard the refrain from fiduciaries that their role was solely to maximize returns, and to force their ESG perspective on the beneficiaries would be highly presumptuous. The concern at the root of this view was that litigious beneficiaries might argue that returns forgone by applying ESG principles are a loss caused by fiduciary decision making. ESG investing was seen as almost a contravention of the fiduciary's duty to act in the beneficiary's best (financial) interests. As the ESG movement has become more widespread, and as the relevant laws have been clarified and tested, this concern has, to some extent, disappeared from the public debate. Put another way, incorporating ESG principles into the investment program is increasingly seen as a core part of the fiduciary's role.[27]

In their own words …

"Funds need to look at the bigger picture, they need to understand that they are investment stewards, they must invest for the longer term, they must understand the intangible risks that can affect the sustainability of an investment or organization, and they must become active in ensuring or at least knowing how those risks are managed across their portfolios— and if it is not right—do something about it."

—Pauline Vamos, former CEO, Regnan, and
independent non-executive director,
Mercer Superannuation (Australia) Limited

Alignment

As suggested by Gandhi, it is reasonable to expect *alignment* between the words and deeds of fiduciaries as they govern the wealth of beneficiaries. To the extent that there is a *dissonance* or inconsistency between promulgated investment beliefs and the management of the pool of wealth, actions will speak louder than the words.

This point introduces a feature of the debate about investment beliefs that we sometimes notice: fiduciaries who appear to profess certain investment beliefs *because they believe they are expected to hold them*, not because they actually do hold them. What should be a firmly held investment belief becomes a form of "virtue signaling" or marketing gimmick. Inevitably, this clash creates the potential for incoherent management actions and mixed signals between fiduciaries and their key stakeholders—beneficiaries, organization managers, asset consultants, and investment managers.

We would argue that it is better to *not have* explicit beliefs than to *fail to act* according to promulgated ones.

---

[27]For an excellent set of resources, see the CFA Institute Future of Finance webpage at www.cfainstitute.org/learning/future/pages/esg.aspx.

We mention alignment between stated beliefs and actions here—and will return to it throughout this book—because echoes of a governing body's investment beliefs should be heard throughout the investment process. If investment beliefs do not have implications, then why hold them in the first place?

For example, if the governing body has a belief that asset allocation is the most important driver of investment outcomes, then a reasonable expectation is that fiduciaries and management will focus much of their attention on this issue. If much of the governing body's (or investment committee's) agenda is focused not on asset allocation but rather on investment selection—for example, so-called beauty parades (see Chapter 7), manager appointments, and approving unlisted investments—then whether the professed investment belief is being "lived out" is questionable. As we will discuss in Chapter 3, an especially important aspect of investment governance is alignment between investment beliefs and both investment objectives and risk preferences. It is through these settings that fiduciaries connect the interests of beneficiaries and the philosophy of the governing body with the concrete objectives given to management to achieve.

Before moving on to Chapter 3, we consider how investment beliefs fit the aviation analogy.

Investment Beliefs and the Airplane Analogy

Suppose we see the aircraft as the investment vehicle, the destination as the investment objective, and the passenger as the beneficiary (say, a defined-contribution [DC] plan member). The passenger's experience is, of course, a function of many factors, including the class of travel and distance, which are, in turn, defined partly by what the airline holds itself out to be.

In the context of the airplane analogy, the closest parallel to investment beliefs would be the strategic approach of the airline's board of directors. For example, a premium international flagship carrier is likely to have new, well-appointed, long-haul aircraft with compelling offerings for first class and business class passengers. Such offerings are how the airline became a successful carrier. In contrast, a short-hop regional carrier is likely to have small, modest aircraft because flying times are shorter, passengers (per flight) fewer, and runways at regional airports are appropriate only for small aircraft. For a premium airline to operate 76-seat Bombardier Q400s on international routes would be as absurd as for a regional airline to operate Airbus A380s with first-class private suites.

The investment organization of a DC plan ("airline") should be aligned with its underlying *raison d'être*, which might be described as achieving retirement security for DC plan members. The governing body can signal how this objective is to be achieved by being clear about its investment beliefs. With this clarity, fiduciaries and management have a common understanding of the strategic context and can seek to fulfill the vision for the plan (airline). Communicated effectively, the vision also signals to stakeholders what the plan offers.

Investment beliefs define the (investment) strategic context for the organization whether it is a DC plan, defined-benefit (DB) plan, endowment, or foundation. Done properly, investment beliefs act as a guiding philosophy ensuring coherence between what the fiduciary decides about the vision for the investment organization, what management does to bring this vision to life, and what the beneficiary ought to expect.

Of course, metaphors have their limitations and, as we promised, we will be clear when the metaphor is being stretched. The attentive reader may have already identified the fact that travelers get to select their preferred airline on the basis of a synthesis of factors, including destination, length of trip, class of travel, loyalty program, and preferred brand. This freedom is not always the case with beneficiaries and the provider of their retirement plan. In practice, at least in the United States, one's retirement plan is usually linked to one's employment relationship; thus, the "airline" is selected for the worker. In Australia, where "choice of fund" legislation enshrines nearly complete portability, a person can select a retirement plan provider (the airline). In practice, despite such portability, default choices (in which a preferred airline is selected by the employer) remain powerful for unknown reasons (Gigerenzer 2008; McKenzie, Liersch, and Finkelstein 2006).

Points for Reflection: Chapter 2. Investment Beliefs: Decision Making in Context

As a fiduciary:

- Do I know my organization's investment beliefs (or principles) or philosophy? Can I list the beliefs or describe the philosophy?

- Do I understand the implications of our investment beliefs or philosophy?

- Does the investment portfolio reflect our investment beliefs or philosophy?

- Do I understand the approach of my organization to investing in relation to ESG factors? Does this approach reflect the views of our beneficiaries?

3. Investment Objectives: What's the Destination?

"A goal *properly set* is halfway reached."

—*Zig Ziglar[28]*

To remind the reader where we are in our *OPERIS* framework, we restate the investment process in **Exhibit 5**. Step O continues to be the focus of our discussion. In Chapter 2, we dealt with only the first consideration in Step O: investment beliefs. By the end of this chapter, you will have covered the key remaining elements for a complete understanding of the underlying investment issue. In the metaphor of the airplane, you will have a detailed

Exhibit 5.   *OPERIS* Framework: Objective, Part 2

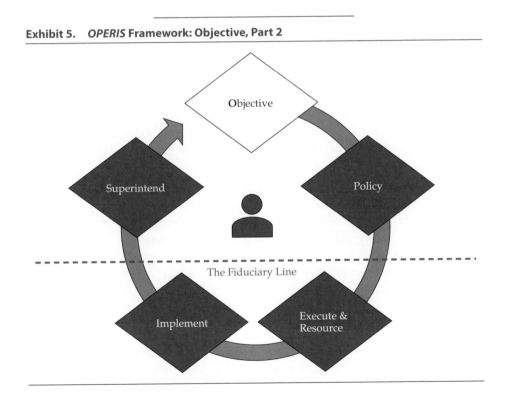

---

[28]Hilary Hinton (Zig) Ziglar (1926–2012) was an American author, salesman, and motivational speaker. See www.ziglar.com/quotes/goals-2/.

understanding of the destination and an understanding of other important factors regarding the nature of the journey.

Before we proceed to the important investment-specific elements of this chapter—investment objectives and risk preferences—we consider certain other factors that influence the context in which investment decisions are made.

Approval and Oversight Processes

To efficiently and effectively conduct an investment process, the governing body must make certain decisions and oversee their implementation. The whole organization must be clear, therefore, about which party approves what and what oversight is required of fiduciaries for them to fulfill their duties under the law. Such processes would usually form part of an organization's overall corporate governance and/or risk management framework. We believe that investment-related approval and oversight processes also must be explicit and documented and that all relevant stakeholders must have the understanding necessary to fulfill their roles in said processes.

The way a governing body exercises oversight and facilitates the necessary approvals to execute investment policy is a function of several factors:

- *Complexity*—Complexity in an investment process can have several sources. For example, the underlying investment issue may itself be complex; that is, the plan may have a significant number of heterogeneous beneficiaries with investment horizons ranging from one day to 45 years. At other plans, complexity may come from the existence of several important stakeholders (e.g., labor unions), each with a critical role to play in investment governance. In yet other cases, complexity may increase with scale, with myriad underlying exposures obtained through a variety of investment vehicles and strategies. Whatever the source of complexity, approval and oversight processes should ensure that the party best equipped to approve or oversee an activity is assigned that responsibility.

- *Governance model*—Although an investor's governance model is usually influenced by the complexity of the overall investment process, fiduciary bodies usually have some latitude to adopt a certain model as long as their fiduciary duties are properly carried out. A centralized, calendar time–based style of investment decision making may be suitable for a simple investment challenge, whereas a relatively complex investment issue or an advanced investment capability may require a delegated, real-time style of investment decision making.[29] In any event, the governance model ought to fit the purpose.

- *Governance budget*—The complexity of the investment arrangements and the governance model typically call for certain governance resources, which are both finite and (relatively) expensive (Clark and Urwin 2008). Therefore, the governance budget ought to be spent in a way that is consistent with the approval and oversight processes determined by the governing body.

- *Legal and regulatory requirements*—Whatever a governing body's view on complexity or the most appropriate governance model, the legal or regulatory requirements must be complied with. In most cases, the law will require what might be described as the bare minimum; thoughtful deliberation about the complexity, model, and budgetary restraints will lead beyond this minimum toward good practice, even best practice.

Instead of recommending a *best model*, as if there were only one, we recommend that the governing body do the following:

- *Deliberate*—The governing body needs to reach some consensus, based on balancing the preceding criteria, about the most appropriate approval and oversight processes. In Chapter 8, we offer the *OPERIS* framework as a way of thinking about how roles and responsibilities are to be allocated.

- *Document*—Once the approval and oversight processes have been agreed upon in principle, the governing body needs to document and approve them through the usual governing body process.

- *Promulgate*—The documented processes should be shared, as needed, with stakeholders, including all those who have a role to play in the investment process, especially those parties with a role above the fiduciary line (i.e., investment committee, management, asset consultants).

- *Reinforce*—Because approval processes are not necessarily referred to regularly, reinforcing the roles of each party in relation to approvals and oversight is beneficial. For example, we know of one governing body that

---

[29]An authoritative source on pension fund governance is Clark and Urwin (2008), in which the authors suggest three governance types: Type 1 sees a board making centralized decisions on a calendar-time basis. Type 3 envisages decision making being delegated (to some degree) by the board to an investment committee and an executive, with the investment committee making calendar-time decisions and the executive making real-time decisions. Type 2 sits somewhere in between, with the investment committee retaining investment decision-making powers.

has a laminated statement of delegations in front of all fiduciaries at all meetings as a convenient point of reference.

- *Revisit*—Finally, as with most policies and processes, reviewing the approval and oversight processes at an agreed interval (say, every one to three years) is desirable to ensure their ongoing appropriateness.

In their own words ...

"Governance takes many shapes for DC plan fiduciaries, whether it's identifying desired participant outcomes, assigning committee responsibilities, or selecting investments. However, one thing is certain: Oversight is critical."

—Lee Freitag, Head of Investment Strategy,
Northern Trust Asset Management

Uses of Entities and Structures

Although some investment organizations involve a single entity with a straightforward legal structure, not all organizations are so simple. Therefore, we recommend that the governing body understand the entities and structures within the organization and make investment decisions with them in mind.

For example, we know of one hybrid pension plan—that is, a plan with elements of both defined-contribution (DC) and defined-benefit (DB) plans—that has both tax-paying and tax-exempt entities and more than one oversight body with (legal or informal) fiduciary duties. Such complexity will dictate how investment objectives are framed, what investment policy is adopted, and how money is invested.

Another circumstance that demands understanding of the entities and structures is the high-net-worth, ultra-high-net-worth, and family office world. In this environment, one or more individuals may be involved in addition to one or more investment trusts. The family may also have a foundation for its charitable activities, and other types of entities may be involved that are jurisdiction specific. For example, Australia makes provision for a vehicle known as the self-managed superannuation fund (SMSF).[30] In a family group, the range of entities and structures may be multiplied horizontally within a generation and vertically between generations. The complexity is almost endless.

The range of complexities may sound daunting, but fiduciaries must grapple with the issues *as they are*, not as they might wish them to be. If the complexity of entities and structures is such that it poses a risk for fiduciaries, that problem must be addressed.

A solution is possible: Such risk can be reduced by, for example, increasing the governance budget or simplifying the range of entities and structures. In extreme cases, the individual fiduciary may decide that the risk is so great that to remain involved is not worth the *career risk*.

Financial Objectives

The investment objective may be but one objective among a range of other *financial* objectives. This book is concerned primarily with investment governance by fiduciaries. Naturally, the investment decision is the primary subject of our attention. Because of circumstances, however, the fiduciary needs to consider the investment decision within a broader context.

For example, the chief financial officer (CFO) of a corporation would most certainly be interested in the ongoing *fundedness* (i.e., the ratio of assets to liabilities) of that corporation's DB plan. The *investment* objective of the DB plan might be described, for example, as "minimizing the probability of underfundedness" (however assets and liabilities are measured[31]). In all likelihood, the CFO is interested in minimizing the probability of a call being made on the corporation to use the corporation's out-of-plan assets to make

---

[30]"Superannuation" refers to a tax-preferred environment providing an incentive for Australians to fully or partially fund their retirement, thus reducing the pressure on public finances. In World Bank terms, "superannuation" can involve mandatory "first" and "second" pillar and voluntary "third" pillar elements (World Bank 2008). As defined by the Australian Securities and Investments Commission, an SMSF is "a private superannuation fund," regulated by the Australian federal taxation authority, that plan members can manage themselves. SMSFs can have up to four members. As Australia's securities regulator notes, "All members must be trustees (or directors if there is a corporate trustee) and are responsible for decisions made about the fund and for complying with relevant laws" (Australian Securities and Investments Commission 2017). For those of means, SMSFs have traditionally been a way of managing taxes (in addition to providing for retirement).

[31]Two possibilities would be the accrued benefits index and the vested benefits index, which are the ratio of the net market value of assets to, respectively, accrued and vested benefits.

good on future shortfalls between pension fund assets and liabilities.[32] When fiduciaries consider a broader financial objective, they *may* approach the investment challenge differently

For another example, consider a wealthy entrepreneur with a significant shareholding in a listed company and a portfolio of financial assets. To focus his attention on the success of the listed business, the entrepreneur has delegated to a fiduciary the role of managing the portfolio of financial assets. How should the fiduciary approach this task? Should he consider the financial assets in a vacuum and seek to maximize risk-adjusted returns? Or consider the entrepreneur's *financial objectives* (and other factors, such as risk preferences) and design the investment strategy for the portfolio of financial assets with the broad financial objectives in mind? Perhaps, the fiduciary may even consider incorporating the entrepreneur's human capital when considering the most appropriate investment strategy for the financial asset portfolio (Bodie, Merton, and Samuelson 1992; Strangeland and Turtle 1999; Milevsky 2009, 2010; Mitchell and Turner 2010). We will return to this example later in this chapter to draw out other relevant points.

Two truisms should be apparent by now:

- These Step O settings are highly interrelated, and they need to be considered comprehensively *before* an investment strategy is resolved.

- This investment governance framework, and the associated process (Exhibit 5), are universal, in that they can be applied to investment issues from pension finance to private wealth management.

Sources and Uses of Funds

Much of finance theory views wealth as a function of returns earned over a given investment horizon and based on a single initial contribution to the portfolio. Cash flows that occur throughout the horizon—like contributions to a DC pension plan—tend to be ignored. Although this assumption may be reasonable when considering one aspect of finance (say, portfolio choice or manager evaluation), it is inaccurate (in the extreme) when considering pension finance and private wealth applications. In this section and the next one, we entertain the idea of *intervening cash flows*. As in the previous section,

---

[32]This factor is one reason behind the rise of DC plans and the demise of DB plans (Drew and Walk 2016). The effect of underfunding has been such an issue for corporations that to avoid this risk, many boards have decided to close DB plans—because they posed too great a risk to their company's balance sheet—and replace them with DC plans, in which the plan participants (consciously or not) take responsibility for financing their retirement (Milevsky and Song 2010).

the elements we consider here, sources and uses of funds, extend beyond the conventional way the investment challenge is defined.

"Sources and uses of funds" refers to cash flows into and out of the investment portfolio from sources or for uses external to the asset vehicles being directly governed by the investment fiduciary. Such sources include, for example, donors in the case of a charitable foundation and the corporate sponsor in the case of a DB plan; uses would typically be payments to beneficiaries. Why might the cash flows to or from these parties be interesting to the fiduciary? Like financial objectives (the previous factor), intervening cash flows *may* affect how the portfolio is designed and managed.

To understand the practical implications of sources and uses of funds, we will revisit the entrepreneur from the previous section. Suppose one of his broad financial objectives is to scratch his entrepreneurial itch by investing cash from his financial portfolio in early-stage venture investments (the timing of which is unknown). Armed with this additional context, the investment fiduciary who takes a holistic view of his principal's best interests may, in concert with the principal, design a financial asset portfolio with slightly lower risk but greater liquidity than previously. The reason is to balance the investor's allocation to relatively risky venture capital investments with a relatively low-risk bond portfolio with easy liquidity. Ready liquidity will enable the investor to promptly fund cash outflows for his venture investments (a *use* of funds).

The reader's reaction may be as follows:

- Why should I (the fiduciary) take into account wealth that is apparently beyond my remit?

- What if the entrepreneur—being a seasoned risk taker—does not want liquid low-risk bonds in the portfolio?

These questions are both reasonable. The concerns most definitely need to be resolved and would naturally be considered if our framework is used as intended. First, to what extent the fiduciary takes into account the beneficiary's (or principal's) entire circumstances depends on such factors as how the fiduciary defines her or his role, what the principal's expectations of the fiduciary's role are, and what the law says about the fiduciary's role. In some cases, the law will oblige an adviser (acting as a fiduciary) to consider the principal's "personal circumstances" (or the legalese equivalent of this formulation). With an entrepreneur such as the one in the example, we see at least two possibilities. The investor could approach the fiduciary for investment advice regarding the financial assets portfolio and explicitly exclude anything else from the scope of the engagement (presumably because he is confident of his abilities to manage the balance of his wealth). Or the investor could engage the fiduciary to consider his wealth in aggregate, thus introducing the possibility of, and the need to consider, sources and uses of funds.

Second, this investor may indeed not wish to proceed with the proposal to hold liquid bonds as a strategy to balance risk and ensure liquidity for cash calls. In practice, the fiduciary would make such a recommendation or take such action only after understanding the principal's investment objectives (as a subset of the investor's financial objectives) and risk preferences. We discuss these two important factors in detail later in this chapter.

For another example, consider a foundation that has been established to fulfill a charitable purpose. The governing body governs the corpus of assets to finance the foundation's spending policy by designing (see Chapter 4) and implementing (see Chapter 7) an appropriate investment policy (see Chapter 5). In this case, the use of funds is to finance the spending policy. If the foundation is subject to a minimum spending rate—typically, 5% of the corpus per year—then the use of funds is likely to affect the investment policy of the foundation. The fiduciaries are left with a choice between targeting an "inflation plus 5%" (or higher) investment objective to maintain the real value of the corpus or setting a lower target and eating into the real value of the corpus. In the economic environment of 2019—in which inflation plus 5% appears to be an ambitious target—this trade-off is real in the minds of many fiduciaries. And we have not even mentioned the risks of this trade-off, which are likely to bias the decision toward the lower return target.

If, as is often the case, the foundation actively raises funds to further its charitable purpose, then donations may be a valuable "source" of funds that builds the foundation's corpus and/or supports an expanded spending policy.

Do not let the specific facts of these examples obscure the point being made: fiduciaries need a clear understanding of the sources and uses of funds they oversee because those factors may affect investment objectives, risk preferences, and investment policies later in the investment process.

Detailed Cash Flow Budgets

To make planning as effective as possible, the ideal approach is, whenever practical, to prepare detailed cash flow budgets (inflows, which will be positive, and outflows, which will be negative) as a prelude to designing the governing body's investment policy. **Exhibit 6** shows a framework for this consideration.

The following simple examples illustrate situations in which detailed cash flow budgets *may* be possible:

- a DB plan estimating future contributions (inflows from working plan members) and pension payments (outflows to retired plan members);

Exhibit 6.   Sources and Uses of Funds and Cash Flows

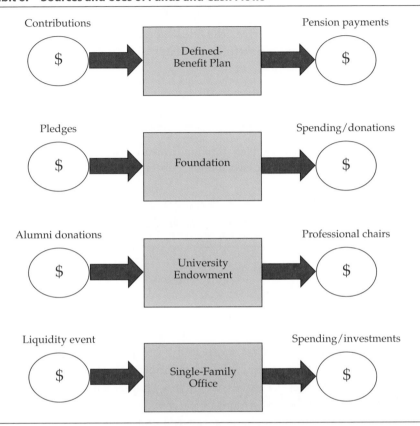

Note: A "liquidity event" would be a cash inflow from, for example, the sale of property.

- a foundation preparing a cash flow budget for pledges (inflows from donors) and spending to fulfill the foundation's charitable purpose (outflows to recipients);

- a university endowment planning for gifts (inflows from, say, alumni) and funding endowed chairs (outflows to university departments and professors); and

- a single-family office anticipating a liquidity event (inflow from the sale of a business or parcel of shares in a business) and planning allowances for family members (outflows to finance the acquisition of Ferraris and super yachts).

The timing, magnitude, and certainty of cash flows—especially inflows—are the variables that make cash flow budgeting difficult and thus introduce additional uncertainty into investment policy development and implementation.

From a textbook perspective, the ideal situation is one in which fiduciaries can design the asset portfolio to match liabilities, thus immunizing against any asset/liability mismatch.

In their own words ...

"[O]nly with appropriate plan design, investments, and communications will a DC participant have a high probability of meeting his or her retirement goals."

—*Josh Cohen, Managing Director,*
Head of Institutional Defined Contribution, PGIM

Investment Objectives

The heart of the investment challenge is to meet the set of investment objectives that, when achieved, define success for the beneficiary. The importance of investment objectives is what motivated us to name the first step in the *OPERIS* framework **O**bjectives. After the importance of objectives is noted, the other aspects of Step O discussed in this chapter provide indispensable additional context for the investment objectives.

Fiduciaries need to be realistic about the challenges they face. First, in most cases, the fiduciary must interpret the investment objectives of the beneficiary on their behalf. Rarely does a fiduciary get the opportunity to confirm the investment objectives of the beneficiaries directly with them for one or both of the following reasons. High levels of *financial literacy* are rare, so the chances of having a fruitful discussion about the beneficiary's investment objectives are remote.[33] In addition, many fiduciaries--for example, DC plan sponsors—will never set eyes on their beneficiaries because the beneficiaries are so numerous and because of the delegated nature of their relationships.

Furthermore, *information asymmetries* make it difficult for the fiduciary to gather enough information to formulate an ideal set of investment objectives for the beneficiary. That is, the fiduciary of a DC plan is likely to observe only a subset of the full set of variables needed to understand the beneficiary's

---

[33]See the important work on financial literacy by Mitchell and Lusardi (2011) and Lusardi and Mitchell (2014).

complete investment challenge. And that statement assumes there is only one beneficiary; in practice, the beneficiaries of most DC plans are a numerous and heterogeneous group of workers. Therefore, assumptions will need to be made about the beneficiaries as a group to make a solution tractable, and even then, it will be only approximately correct. Only in certain circumstances do fiduciaries understand the full details of the beneficiary's circumstances; such a circumstance would involve a financial planner and her client.[34]

Finally, the terms in which the investment challenge is expressed are important. Because this study is principally focused on *investment governance*, the temptation is to launch into a technical discussion expressed in terms familiar to investment professionals—"inflation plus 5%" or "maximizing the portfolio's Sharpe ratio." Indeed, because investment specialists are usually the ones who generate investment recommendations for fiduciaries, the conversation at the fiduciary board level can become narrowly focused on investment specifics rather than on how investment policies and results affect beneficiaries.[35]

The best way to change this emphasis is for fiduciary bodies to express investment objectives in a way that *both* they and their beneficiaries can understand. For example, instead of "inflation plus 5%," fiduciaries might select a headline investment objective such as "maximizing the likelihood of replacing 70% of preretirement income."

Framing investment objectives in this way has several benefits. First, every person can understand this objective. Everyone with a calculator can compute what 70% of their current salary is and can, with a little budget thinking, come to some sort of conclusion about the adequacy of such an income. Few

---

[34]A cynic might call into question this statement. One critique of the typical financial planner/client relationship goes as follows: Financial planners learn as much as they need to know about their clients to demonstrate a legal standard of due diligence and then provide an investment solution based on the clients' risk tolerances. Because financial planners are increasingly compensated by fees only (not by fees based on assets under management), the best way to maximize the margin on each marginal client is to minimize the amount of time spent on that client. Again, we see an example of the tension identified by Ellis (2011). This example is not intended to reflect poorly on all financial planners. In our experience, a growing number of financial planners are taking their commitments to clients very seriously indeed.

[35]The pure investment orientation of many discussions at the fiduciary board has other negative side effects. For example, some important variables in pensions finance—such as contributions—tend to be overlooked in favor of investment issues, such as changing asset allocations, new managers, or new investment selections. In some cases, fiduciaries might be better served by recommending that plan members increase contributions instead of increasing investment risk. In our pessimistic moments, we wonder whether such considerations ever really get a fair hearing. A comprehensive understanding and examination of the dynamics of retirement investing is necessary to make effective decisions on behalf of beneficiaries.

---

individuals other than investment professionals are capable of translating an "inflation plus" investment objective, expressed as an annual rate of return on the dollar amount invested, into an equivalent sustainable retirement income.

Second, the objective of a 70% replacement rate is expressed as income, which is how the average person thinks about finances. Converting an estimated final account balance—technically, estimated wealth at time T—into a sustainable income is also beyond the financial skills of most people.

Third, income replacement at a certain level—in this case, 70%—is a measure that is at the same time universal and specific. It is universal in that "70% income replacement" can be applied to everyone, no matter what their wealth or occupation; it is specific in that it targets a *level* of income that is a function of preretirement earnings, which the literature shows to be an important driver of expectations about retirement income (Baker, Logue, and Rader 2004; Basu and Drew 2010).

Fourth, the objective as stated is expressed in *probabilistic terms*. This approach is important as a communication tool because it gives the beneficiary a sense that, although 70% income replacement is the target, this level might not be achieved. It is misleading to leave the beneficiary with the impression that any reasonable investment objective can be achieved with certainty.[36]

Finally, the framing of this investment objective can be used to motivate action on the part of the beneficiary. For example, a DC plan might report in its communication with plan members that the "probability of replacing 70% of preretirement income" is 50%—the toss of a fair coin. Rather than leaving the information at that, the DC plan could use this estimate and the plan member's reaction to it to drive positive retirement investing behavior, such as suggesting that members

- contribute more to raise the probability of achieving the objective;

- take more, or a different type of, investment risk to raise the probability of achieving the objective;[37]

- defer the retirement date to raise the probability of achieving the objective by accumulating more retirement savings during the additional working

---

[36]By buying laddered portfolios of US Treasury Inflation-Protected Securities or inflation-linked annuities, a retirement outcome can be more or less guaranteed, but such approaches are expensive (in terms of the amount that needs to be saved).

[37]This lever is overused, however, relative to the others because investment professionals tend to dominate investment discussions among governing boards. Also, this lever allows the investment industry to come up with innovative solutions or silver bullets that they assert will "add value." In short, this course of action is good for "the economics of the business" (Ellis 2011).

years and shortening the retirement phase (assuming the date of death in the calculation remains constant); and

- seek personal financial advice.[38]

In translating the investment problem into a set of investment objectives, fiduciaries would do well to keep in mind the following circumstances:

- *Multiple, competing objectives*—We have encountered few examples of fiduciaries having in mind a single, all-encompassing investment objective that adequately distills the investment need. In practice, the fiduciary faces multiple objectives of the beneficiary(ies), including projected retirement incomes, return targets, risk expressed multiple ways, fee budgets, and so on. In almost every case, the set of investment objectives involves trade-offs. The trade-offs contained in the investment objective *must* be explicitly identified and understood by fiduciaries.

- *Objectives needing to be prioritized*—Because trade-offs exist, the hierarchy of objectives must be clarified. Priorities, provided they are shared by all beneficiaries, greatly assist in making on-balance and marginal decisions.

- *Stated versus revealed objectives and priorities*—Sometimes the stated priorities of fiduciary bodies conflict with the priorities revealed by their actual behavior. For example, in Australia, where near-universal portability results in a significant focus on "league tables" (i.e., rankings of pension funds by realized return), fiduciary bodies seem to think that ranking *peer-relative* performance too high in the order of priorities sends the wrong signal to plan members about the importance of absolute performance. Therefore, they tend to rank absolute performance higher than peer-relative performance in their *stated* objectives. This choice is completely defensible, but it is a good practice if and only if the stated objectives are the governing body's *real* objectives. The risk is that the *revealed* objectives—the ones focused on around the fiduciary table—may be different from the stated ones. For example, in this case, the fiduciaries may act strongly to reward good peer-relative performance. We recommend

---

[38]We are often asked to provide our view about what is "the best" way to achieve retirement adequacy for plan members. Whatever the audience, the answer is for plan members to obtain (and follow!) high-quality personal financial advice. We usually follow this statement with some clarifying points. For example, the proportion of plan members who seek personal financial advice is low; therefore, DC plan fiduciaries have an important part to play in at least positively influencing retirement outcomes. Our point also underlines the importance of the availability of high-quality personal financial advice. In many jurisdictions, the need for high-quality financial advice is driving the focus of policymakers on financial planner competence and incentives (especially avoiding perverse ones).

that the governing body honestly deliberate over and document its objective set with the goal of setting clear marching orders for management.

While we may have made the process sound straightforward, objective setting brings with it some challenges, as follows:

- *Objectives that change*—In a perfect world, investment objectives ought to remain relatively constant over time. In practice, reasons may arise for introducing new objectives or priorities may change. While we advocate making sure that the officially promulgated investment objectives are complete and accurate at all times, we also counsel against their being changed too often. Significant changes in investment objectives may result in equally significant changes to the investment program, with negative side effects (such as transaction costs and other costs associated with turnover).

- *Interaction with market conditions*—A common reason for changes in investment objectives is prevailing *market conditions*. For example, when markets become more volatile, risk-related investment objectives tend to increase in importance in the minds of fiduciaries. Discipline among fiduciaries is required to differentiate between permanent changes in investment objectives—which should be relatively rare—and short-term responses to market conditions. Mistaking the short term for the long term may send confusing signals to stakeholders (especially management).

- *Future expectations*—Objectives are usually developed, at least in part, on the basis of previous experience. The future, however, may be materially different from the past (see Bianchi, Drew, and Walk 2016a), which may require change in objectives. Fiduciaries are encouraged to make their objectives as achievable as possible to avoid setting unrealistic expectations among stakeholders and/or inducing actions counterproductive to the interests of beneficiaries. For example, fiduciaries are currently faced with the choice between maintaining arguably unrealistic return targets—say, inflation plus 5% per annum—and taking the associated high level of investment risk or lowering return targets and reducing the probability of achieving the retirement income expectations of beneficiaries.

- *Agency risk*—Whatever objectives fiduciaries choose, the risk remains that the objectives are inappropriate for at least some beneficiaries. Given the size and heterogeneity of some groups of beneficiaries—for example, the plan members of a public DC plan—this risk is to be expected. We recommend that fiduciaries combine a range of measures to ensure that the interests of all beneficiaries are served. For example, fiduciaries can create well-designed age-based defaults with clever design features, such as *auto-escalation* features, but also provide plan members access to financial advice in case beneficiaries need a different design. Whatever course of action the governing body decides to take, the agreed investment objectives should focus on measurable investment aspects of the offering. Other elements of the offering—such as how best to deliver personal financial advice to plan members (e.g., face-to-face, telephone, or robo-advice)—can and should be discussed during broader product and service deliberations.

The final element of our discussion of investment objectives is a tool that assists fiduciaries with marginal decision making. How might fiduciaries compare the expected outcomes from two (or more) competing investment strategies in the context of the multiple, competing objectives we have discussed? The answer is the *hierarchy of investment objectives* (HIO), an example of which is shown in **Exhibit 7**.[39]

As the reader has no doubt realized, the HIO is merely an expedient for recording and prioritizing the investment objectives that, in the fiduciary's view, *best capture* the essence of the underlying investment problem. Obviously, framing, agreeing, and prioritizing is the difficult task; recording the objectives is trivial. We think presentation of the HIO is important, however, because good presentation can assist decision making as much as poor presentation can hamper it.

An HIO is only as good as the criteria within it, and the analysis that underlies it. If the HIO criteria (i.e., the investment objectives) are mis-specified or the analysis is deficient, the inferences drawn from the HIO and the decisions made will be incorrect. In this chapter, we have discussed some issues to consider when resolving investment objectives in the form of HIO criteria. In Chapter 4, we discuss how the HIO drives portfolio choice.

---

[39]As with the investment process we introduced earlier in this study, this tool is not original. We have come across various versions of it in our professional travels in financial services and beyond, mainly in the form of a balanced scorecard (which builds on the work of scholars such as Kaplan and Norton 1992). A cursory examination of the range of scorecards available via the internet reveals they are used for many different purposes. We have selected one we believe best summarizes the task at hand—using a prioritization of investment objectives as a tool for decision making. In particular, we would like to acknowledge the following organizations and their past and present staff: the Myer Family Company, QSuper, QIC and Equipsuper. Through our work at and with these organizations, and through our work with individuals who worked at these organizations, we have developed and improved this tool to its current form.

Exhibit 7. Hierarchy of Investment Objectives

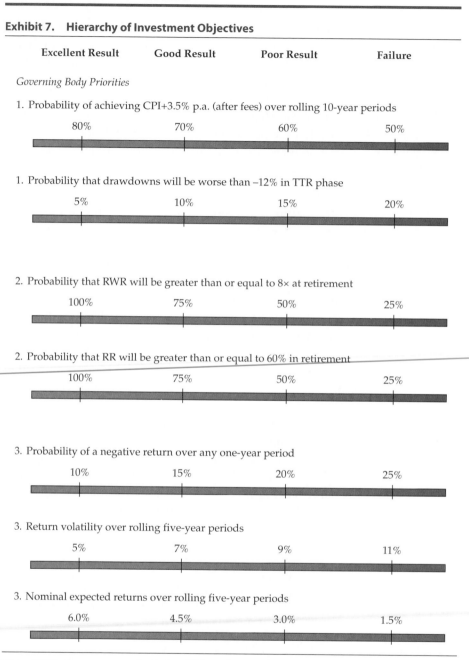

Excellent Result	Good Result	Poor Result	Failure

Governing Body Priorities

1. Probability of achieving CPI+3.5% p.a. (after fees) over rolling 10-year periods

  80%   70%   60%   50%

1. Probability that drawdowns will be worse than –12% in TTR phase

  5%   10%   15%   20%

2. Probability that RWR will be greater than or equal to 8× at retirement

  100%   75%   50%   25%

2. Probability that RR will be greater than or equal to 60% in retirement

  100%   75%   50%   25%

3. Probability of a negative return over any one-year period

  10%   15%   20%   25%

3. Return volatility over rolling five-year periods

  5%   7%   9%   11%

3. Nominal expected returns over rolling five-year periods

  6.0%   4.5%   3.0%   1.5%

Notes: CPI is the consumer price index; TTR is the transition to retirement phase; RWR is retirement wealth ratio; RR is replacement rate.

Risk Preferences

The classical approach in finance sees risk preferences as largely a function of risk tolerance. According to this view, the risk a fiduciary ought to take for an individual or organization should be the maximum that the individual or organization can reasonably tolerate. Such an approach appears to neatly match the typical approach to investing, which views wealth maximization as the desirable outcome; that is, individuals will seek to maximize wealth in light of their personal risk tolerance.

In practice, we observed two particular manifestations of this focus on risk tolerance.

First, *DC plan members* have responsibility for their own retirement outcomes and, therefore, must themselves make investment decisions (guided or not) to secure their own retirement. DC plan fiduciaries usually make available to plan members a menu of options. Historically, these have been "target risk" in nature; that is, the option's investment strategy is designed to target a given level of risk, and the label gives the plan member some intuition about the option's risk profile (e.g., "conservative" or "aggressive"). Recently, fiduciaries have extended the range of options to "target date" or "life-cycle" options, in which the amount of risk depends on the plan member's time to retirement. This development is an implicit recognition that investing for an individual's retirement is a much more complex problem than target risk–style investment options might lead one to believe.

Second, when an individual becomes a client of a financial planner, one of the first things the person is typically asked to do is complete a risk questionnaire. Such questionnaires are supposed to translate the client's responses into some sort of risk profile that is consistent with that client's predisposition to risk. When taken together with the client's personal circumstances (hopefully!), this risk profile leads to a recommended investment strategy.

Good reasons may support an approach driven by risk tolerance—for example, it arguably minimizes *capitulation risk* (i.e., selling after a drawdown) by matching portfolio risk to risk attitude. Some fairly significant questions remain, however, about a risk-tolerance-only approach

- *Stability of risk tolerance measures*—While the evidence for and against the stability of risk tolerance measures remains mixed, those that advocate for the importance of risk tolerance—e.g., purveyors of risk questionnaires—acknowledge that "risk behavior will be a function of a number of factors, the one most relevant to behavior during market turmoil being risk perception" (Davey 2012).[40] To us the argument seems a little self-defeating; risk tolerance is an important indicator, but "risk behavior" is much more complex than just risk tolerance.

- *Other factors*—We argue that other aspects of risk are important to achieving investment objectives. We discuss this view in further detail below.

- *Real rationale*—We sometimes wonder whether the rationale for the focus on risk tolerance is to serve the interests of the client or plan member, on the one hand, or, instead, the interests of the financial planning firm or DC plan on the other hand? This question provides an excellent illustration of the tension between the "the economics of the business" and "the values of the profession" (Ellis 2011). Risk questionnaires allow financial planners an efficient, evidence-based mechanism for matching clients to a small number of off-the-shelf investment strategies (so-called model portfolios). That the mechanism is evidence based means the financial planner has undertaken some due diligence; that it is efficient means that the returns to scale are greater as a result of little client-by-client tailoring. Because true tailoring is time consuming and, therefore, expensive, the financial planner—or her employer—has a strong incentive to industrialize the process to the greatest extent possible. In short, risk questionnaires are good for the "economics" of the business because they neatly sift a heterogeneous client base into a small number of (hopefully, well-governed) model portfolios. But do risk questionnaires really demonstrate the "values" of the profession by seeking to devise the best financial plan to address the idiosyncratic investment objectives of real, human clients? For the sake of clients, we hope they do, but we wonder.

As we have stated, we believe a beneficiary's risk profile should consider aspects of risk beyond risk tolerance. Our preferred characterization reflects the work of Davey (2015), as shown pictorially in **Exhibit 8**.

The model in Exhibit 8 deems a beneficiary's risk profile to be a balance of three competing aspects of risk:

1. *Risk required*—Depending on the beneficiary's circumstances, investment risk will play a greater or lesser part in achieving the person's goals. Risk required is a judgment about the financial risk that *needs* to be assumed

---

[40]Some research has suggested that risk tolerance is unstable (e.g., Yao, Hanna, and Lindamood 2004), although in some cases these findings have been revisited and clarified (Hanna and Lindamood 2009). Other research suggests that financial risk tolerance is a "genetic and predispositional stable personality trait and, as such, is highly unlikely to change over the life of an individual" (Van de Venter, Michayluk, and Davey 2012, p. 800]).

Exhibit 8.   Risk Profile

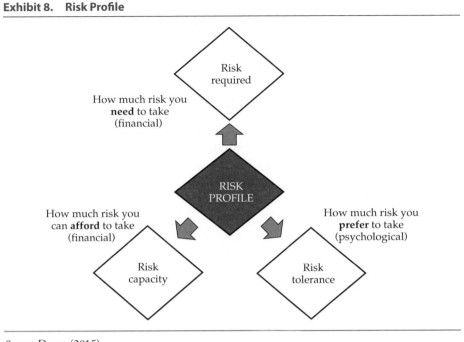

How much risk you **need** to take (financial) — Risk required

How much risk you can **afford** to take (financial) — Risk capacity

RISK PROFILE

How much risk you **prefer** to take (psychological) — Risk tolerance

Source: Davey (2015).

to have a reasonable probability of achieving the agreed set of investment objectives. Importantly, risk required might be different from the level of risk implied by a beneficiary's risk capacity or risk tolerance.

2. *Risk capacity*—The beneficiary's overall financial situation will indicate the level of risk the person can *afford* to take in pursuit of the objective. Risk capacity is, at its core, a judgment about the ability of the client to withstand negative events (e.g., lower or negative contributions because of sudden job loss).

3. *Risk tolerance*—As discussed, risk tolerance is an indication of the amount of risk a person *prefers* to take. In this context, we assume that risk tolerance is a psychological predisposition that is relatively constant over time.

These aspects of risk compete with each other in that they often tend to send opposite signals about what the beneficiary's risk profile ought to be. To bring to life these mixed signals, and the trade-off that results, let us consider two examples.

First, consider a career public employee with modest personal assets in addition to his residence and his DC plan account. Typically, such a worker will use systematic withdrawals from his DC plan to finance his retirement spending (Milevsky 2012; Vernon 2012; Drew and Walk 2015). In such a case, the worker will usually need to take moderate-to-high levels of investment risk to generate a sufficiently large retirement income; thus, his *risk required* will be relatively high. But such a worker might also have a relatively low *risk tolerance*; after all, he has selected a career that has relatively secure tenure and, as Milevsky (2009) might say, bondlike cash flows. This secure job tenure will likely result in great certainty that he will be able to contribute more to his DC plan than he currently is because as he enters his late 50s and early 60s, other spending commitments—such as raising and educating children—will decrease. In other words, his *risk capacity* may be significant. Note that one of these aspects of risk—risk tolerance—is suggesting a more modest risk profile, whereas the other two aspects—risk required and risk capacity—point in the other direction.

Second, consider a self-made ultra-high-net-worth individual. With significant net worth, such a person may not need to take much risk to meet her financial commitments (even if those commitments are more significant than an average person's). For this individual, a low-risk portfolio might produce enough income to pay the bills as well as allow saving for significant wealth. So, *risk required* is low. Because our hypothetical individual is self-made, however, she is likely to have generated her wealth by taking significant business and/or financial risks. Therefore, her *risk tolerance* is probably high—certainly higher than that of the average person. Similarly, because of her significant wealth, she may be able to afford to take significant financial risks, which suggests a high *risk capacity*. In this case, then, we also see a tension between the three aspects of risk. Two aspects are pointing to a risk profile that is high risk, and the third aspect points in the opposite direction.

The key lesson from these examples is that, as with setting investment objectives, resolving a risk profile is not always simple; ultimately, it requires some sort of trade-off.

Note that each of the preceding aspects of risk is *endogenous* to the investment issue; that is, each aspect is judged with respect to the beneficiary's situation as though the investment world did not exist. No consideration of *exogenous* risk, such as prevailing risk levels in a given market, has been made.[41]

This distinction is important. The risk preferences discussed here are only about the investment challenges facing the fiduciary, and this discussion

---

[41]An example of prevailing risk levels in a given market is the CBOE (Chicago Board Options Exchange) Volatility Index (the VIX), which is "a key measure of market expectations of near-term volatility conveyed by S&P 500 stock index option prices" (CBOE 2017). As such, it is exogenous to the fiduciary's investment decision, although market volatility doubtless has a bearing on risk attitudes among the beneficiaries fiduciaries seek to serve.

should necessarily be about the beneficiaries and what is in their interests. The fiduciary might also have a belief, or set of considerations, about *exogenous* risk. For example, the fiduciary might believe—as we suggest in the second belief in Chapter 1—that markets are dynamic, and that risk is, as a result, time varying. Such a view ought not impact on the risk preferences of the beneficiary as discussed in this chapter, but it may have implications in other parts of the investment process, such as the desirability of a dynamic asset allocation process and the need to commit resources sufficient to properly implement such an approach.

Having completed our consideration of Step O in the investment process, in Chapter 4, we start to grapple with the issues associated with *solving* the investment problem.

Points for Reflection: Chapter 3. Investment Beliefs: What's the Destination?

As a fiduciary:

- Are approval and oversight processes appropriate in light of the complexity, governance model, governance budget, and legal and regulatory requirements of the organization?

- Do I understand who makes which investment decisions? Are approval and oversight processes, including any delegations (to, say, implemented consultants), documented and monitored?

- Do I have a clear understanding of the entities and structures at play at my investment organization and how they may influence investment decision making?

- Am I aware of all other financial objectives (if any) that may influence the investment decision?

- Do I have a complete understanding of the sources and uses of funds that will influence the investment decision? Have I considered the need for detailed cash flow budgets?

- Can I accurately define "the destination": the critical investment objectives, in order of priority, that correctly and comprehensively summarize the investment problem?

- Am I prepared to make trade-offs in achieving critical investment objectives?

- Am I comfortable that beneficiaries understand this destination (i.e., the critical investment objectives)? Are they likely to understand the terms in which the destination is expressed?

- Do I ensure that new investment ideas are evaluated in light of "the destination?" For example, are those who make investment recommendations required to show that any new recommendation will result in an improved journey to the destination?

- Do I have a clear understanding of the risk preferences of beneficiaries?

4. Portfolio Choice: Getting to the Destination

"Our goals can only be reached through a vehicle of *a plan*, in which we must fervently believe, and upon which we must vigorously act. There is no other route to success."

—*Pablo Picasso[42] (emphasis added)*

In Chapters 2 and 3, we discussed a range of contextual issues that affect investment objectives, such as investment beliefs, and how to identify and enunciate investment objectives that represent the way the governing body interprets the underlying investment challenge. In this chapter, we leave Step O and move to Step P, **P**olicy, in the *OPERIS* framework, which is highlighted in **Exhibit 9**.

Exhibit 9. *OPERIS* Framework: Policy, Part 1

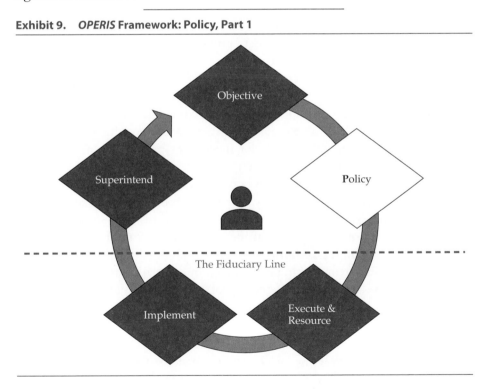

[42]Picasso (1881–1973) was a Spanish painter, sculptor, printmaker, ceramicist, poet, and playwright. This quote is often attributed to Picasso; see https://www.pablopicasso.org/quotes.jsp.

Step P, **P**olicy, relates the "how" to the "what" of objectives. In other words, Step O told us what the fiduciary sets out to achieve for beneficiaries; Step P outlines, in the form of a policy (or what Picasso called "a plan"), *how* the objectives will be achieved.

Portfolio Choice under Uncertainty

As Merton (1997) put it in his Nobel Prize lecture, financial economics is a discipline principally concerned with the "allocation and deployment of economic resources, both spatially and across time, in an uncertain environment." Simply put, financial economics, or finance, is the study of decision making under uncertainty and across time. The reader will notice from these definitions that decision making under uncertainty is precisely what the fiduciary faces in Step P of the *OPERIS* framework. How does the fiduciary allocate wealth—on behalf of beneficiaries—among the range of investment propositions to achieve the investment objectives outlined and prioritized in the hierarchy of investment objectives (HIO)?

When it comes to this investment decision—or, in formal terms, portfolio choice—we can rely on one of the most famous financial theorists for the guiding philosophy—namely, the pioneering work of Markowitz (1952). His seminal work presenting the basics of modern portfolio theory was the first formal treatment of the benefits of portfolio diversification. The work showed that by constructing a portfolio of imperfectly correlated assets, one can reduce portfolio risk for a given level of expected return. Since Markowitz, diversification has remained the essential principle for investment practice, even though the weaknesses of diversification have been acknowledged and the literature has advanced.[43] As we will see later in this book, the classical asset-class approach to diversification is but one potential way of framing an investment policy.

Research has shown that the portfolio choice decision—that is, asset allocation—is responsible for a significant portion of total portfolio outcomes. Depending on the authority one refers to, up to 90% of the differences between portfolio outcomes can be explained by asset allocation.[44] This fact is important for two reasons. First, because of its importance, this chapter will focus primarily on portfolio choice and how to use asset allocation to achieve the investment objectives. And, second, and most notably for the fiduciary

---

[43]As examples of discussions of weaknesses, see the debate on the diversification delta by Vermorken, Medda, and Schröder (2012) and Flores, Bianchi, Drew, and Trück (2017). The common critique of diversification is that its main benefit—spreading of risk—tends to disappear during periods of market dislocation, such as the financial crisis of 2007–2008. In such market environments, realized correlations rise and most (if not all) asset prices fall in unison.
[44]See Brinson et al. (1986), Ibbotson and Kaplan (2000), Statman (2001), and Scott et al. (2017).

reader, the importance of asset allocation gives a strong hint to what ought to be the focus of the marginal governance hour.

The governance budget is a limited resource that needs to be devoted to activities that result in better outcomes for beneficiaries. If one believes the research that 80%–90% of portfolio outcomes are the result of asset allocation, then does the governing body devote 8 out of every 10 minutes to this decision? Or is time best spent on investment manager beauty parades, discussing the latest hedge fund strategy, or poring over slickly presented PowerPoint slides? From an investment governance perspective, when contrasted with the asset allocation decision, these other activities are so low in value added (in a *relative* sense) that they should be delegated to staff members who have the time and expertise to properly evaluate the claims made.[45] We grapple with these issues and related questions in this chapter.

What Is "Optimality"?

Before explaining how we link the asset allocation decision to the HIO, we will define some terms. The word "optimality" can be used in at least two senses. The first is technical. In a Markowitzian paradigm, an optimal portfolio is the one that, given a set of assumptions and constraints, provides the mathematically determined best trade-off of expected reward for risk.[46] Variations on Markowitz (1952) tend to revolve around how the risk aspect of this trade-off is measured. For example, Xiong and Idzorek (2011) evaluated "optimal" mean-conditional value-at-risk (CVaR) portfolios for several levels of expected return.[47] The authors compared this approach to the Markowitz mean–variance equivalents. Markowitz optimality in other settings depends on one or more of the following factors: the assumption set, the constraints applied, and/or the target levels of return or risk. Whatever the case, the first sense of the word "optimality" is mathematical and precise.

Optimality in its second sense—the one for which we have more sympathy in the context of this study—is of the qualitative, judgmental variety. The governing body must *interpret* the investment challenge facing the beneficiary and *enunciate* it in the form of investment objectives that are *documented* and

---

[45]In making this statement, we are assuming that the fiduciary is not an investment expert, which is, in our experience, true—particularly in our dealings with DC plans.

[46]One problem with this interpretation of optimality is that, because it is mathematically determined, it has the appearance of precision. In practice, the results of such optimization routines are highly sensitive to assumptions and constraints.

[47]CVaR defines risk as left-tail risk; that is, this measure acknowledges that substantial negative returns loom large in the minds of most investors and are particularly damaging to portfolio wealth (especially in a pension finance paradigm).

55

prioritized in the form of the HIO. Because no objective interpretation of the investment issue exists (i.e., it was not handed down on tablets of stone), two fiduciaries could view optimality differently and define and prioritize the investment objectives quite differently from each other. The qualitative and judgmental aspects of this second view of optimality need not be a problem as long as the governing body has a process for translating objectives into an appropriate asset allocation and for making marginal decisions. We present just such a process in the next section of this chapter.

Optimality understood in this second sense is, in our view, the most appropriate and honest way of grappling with multiple objectives. The fiduciary has the option to hide the complexity of the investment issue behind a caricature of it—such as to "maximize the Sharpe ratio"[48]—or to confront the complexity head on by identifying the multiple, sometimes competing, objectives and seeking the best trade-off. What this approach may lack in mathematical elegance, we argue, it makes up for in realism. What is sought is the asset allocation that maximizes the probability of achieving the governing body's investment objectives.

As for realism, the process outlined in the next section is founded on certain preferences:

- *Parametric versus nonparametric methods*—In a world of plentiful data, we would prefer to use nonparametric methods to conduct all financial modeling because the richness of the data is retained (rather than being lost in the process of parameterization).[49] Regrettably, such a world does not exist, and with the ongoing emergence of new asset classes and investment propositions, the problem of data scarcity is getting worse, not better. We are thus left with parametric methods. Because of the extensive evidence regarding the empirical distributions of financial returns, in the

---

[48]There is nothing wrong with the Sharpe ratio if one knows the implications of using it as the basis for selecting an optimal portfolio. The main argument in favor of the Sharpe ratio is the fact that it is a reward-for-risk measure (see Sharpe 1966) and, therefore, explicitly recognizes both sides of the investment coin (return and risk). The measure has several weaknesses, however, when used naively. For example, it is a return-only measure—that is, it does not capture other variables that matter in retirement investing, such as contributions and compounding. Also, the risk measure used in the denominator—standard deviation—is a measure of volatility that treats upside and downside variation equally. In reality, volatility above the mean is not really what nonfinance people have in mind when they think of risk.

[49]"Parameterization" is reducing a full data set to a small list of statistical attributes, such as mean, standard deviation, and correlation.

analysis that follows, we use parametric methods that permit the use of the higher moments—that is, skewness and kurtosis.[50]

- *Multiple techniques (unconstrained and constrained)*—To build a rich picture of the portfolio choice problem, to validate the modeling output, and to observe the impact of constraints on results, we consider seven portfolio selection techniques. They range from pure Markowitz mean–variance optimization to target-CVaR optimization in both unconstrained and constrained variations.

- *Simulation techniques*—The essence of decision making under uncertainty is our lack of knowledge about the future. To understand how the "optimal" portfolio might perform in the future, we use simulation techniques that generate synthetic return paths that can be analyzed. With a sense about how competing strategies might perform in the future, we can evaluate which strategy might be superior at meeting the investment objectives set by the governing body.

- *Flexible outputs*—As time passes, and the academic and practitioner literature evolves, new measures, analytical tools, and visualization techniques emerge. Ultimately, these methods seek to turn raw data and analytics into insight and effective decisions. Therefore, we developed the models

---

[50]Much of finance (and economic) theory—including the modern portfolio theory of Markowitz—is based on a range of simplifying assumptions that make the underlying models tractable and implementable. One such assumption is the traditional, but much criticized, use of the normal (or Gaussian) probability distribution. Granger (2005), for example, noted that "much of early econometrics used . . . a Gaussian assumption simply for mathematical convenience and without proper testing" (p. 17). Vocal critics include Taleb (2004, 2007), who asserted, for example, that the normal distribution misrepresents risks posed by fat tails on the left (negative) side of the distribution. A Gaussian distribution can be described with two parameters—the mean and the variance. By characterizing the distribution of asset returns in the first moment (mean) and second moment (variance), the analyst is implicitly accepting that the distribution of all individual assets in the portfolio (and, therefore, the joint distribution) is Gaussian and that mean and variance are sufficient to describe the entire distribution of each portfolio asset. Empirical research has shown that such assumptions are not reasonable and that other distributions—for example, the stable Paretian distribution (Mandelbrot 1963, 1967; Fama 1965)—are superior. The stable Paretian is offered as a superior alternative because "in contrast to the normal distribution, which is symmetric and cannot account for the heavy-tailed nature of returns of financial variables, the class of nonnormal stable distributions has skewed and heavy-tailed representatives" (Rachev, Stoyanov, and Fabozzi 2008, p. 120). A significant amount of research in finance has focused on understanding and properly characterizing empirical return distributions and developing quantitative methods that improve analysis and decisions. To account for the "skewed and heavy-tailed" nature of return distributions, we use techniques that allow the third moment (skewness) and fourth moment (kurtosis) to be specified for each eligible asset class.

57

so that the outputs would be highly flexible and could be presented in numerous ways to appeal to diverse groups of fiduciaries.

Like the investment beliefs outlined in Chapter 2, by listing these preferences, we seek neither to convince the reader that they must follow such a path, nor to imply that they represent the only worldview one might hold. We have two goals: first, we want to give fiduciaries a sense of some of the choices embedded in the analysis they consider when making portfolio choices, and second, we wish to present the main *lessons learned* from our time as scholars and practitioners. As Otto von Bismarck—the 19th-century Prussian statesman and early pioneer of pensions—is thought to have said, "Only a fool learns from [their] own mistakes. The wise [person] learns from the mistakes of others."

Having provided some background about portfolio choice and the way we prefer to approach it, we now turn to our process within the process to identify the optimal asset allocation for a specific governing body's HIO.

A Process within the Process

To generate an asset allocation and complete the essential parts of the Step P in the *OPERIS* framework, we follow the seven steps in the investment process shown in **Exhibit 10**.

To begin, we draw the reader's attention to Step 5, Exhibit 10, denoted "Hierarchy of Investment Objectives." The HIO is the mechanism for linking the investment policy development process—which we are about to discuss—to the governing body's interpretation of the beneficiary's underlying investment challenge, which we discussed in Chapters 2 and 3. We set out to

Exhibit 10.   The Investment Process

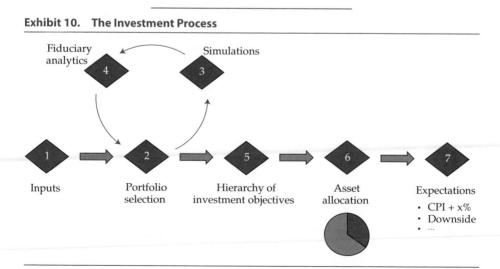

identify, using a rigorous, systematic approach, the optimal investment policy or asset allocation (see Step 6, Exhibit 10), where "optimal" is used in the "qualitative, judgmental" sense. Moreover, we seek to identify the policy in a way that is in complete alignment with the settings agreed to by the fiduciaries in Step O of the *OPERIS* framework. For example, if the governing body has a documented investment belief that passive management of, say, large-capitalization equities is to be preferred, then the assumptions to be developed in Step 1, Exhibit 10, would apply to a large-cap equity index fund.[51]

Now consider each of the seven steps in this process within a process in turn.

Step 1: Inputs. An important element of any investment policy is the list of eligible asset classes and investments, sometimes known as the "opportunity set." **Exhibit 11** provides an example opportunity set. In the simplest

Exhibit 11. Illustrative Asset-Class Opportunity Set

Growth Assets	Defensive Assets	Alternative Assets

• Domestic equities
  • By capitalization
  • Factor investing
• Global equities
  • Developed market equities
    —By region, by country
  • Emerging market equities
    —By region, by country
 	
• Private equity
  • Buyouts
  • Venture capital
	• Fixed interest
	  • Inflation-linked bonds
	  • Sovereign bonds
	  • Corporate bonds
	• Cash
		• Real estate
		  • Commercial
		  • Industrial
		  • Office
		• Timberland
		• Farmland
		• Infrastructure
		• Private loans
		• Hedge funds
		• Commodities
		• Insurance-linked
		  securities (includes
		  catastrophe bonds)
		• Intellectual property funds

Notes: This opportunity set is illustrative only. We expect that more than one of these categorizations would be cause for debate. For example, in Australia, real estate is not usually categorized as an alternative asset. Also, some asset classes are so broad that they could reasonably fit into all categories. "Infrastructure" assets, for example, can be extremely growth oriented (like private equity), can be defensive (like inflation-linked bonds), or can provide alternative return drivers.

---

[51]We are not expressing a view about passive management. We are merely highlighting that investment beliefs have implications throughout the process. If they do not have implications, they are not investment beliefs. By way of example, some of our clients believe in a skill premium for large capitalization equities and add their targeted value-added to the expected asset class return.

of investment portfolios, such asset classes would be limited to stocks (or equities), bonds (or fixed income/fixed interest), and cash (or Treasury bills). In more complex investment portfolios, the number of asset classes can grow to a dozen or more as investors seek new and attractive sources of return and diversification. Some of the more exotic asset classes could include insurance-linked securities and intellectual property funds.

Asset classes themselves include subordinate classes. For example, equity investments may be viewed granularly by geography (e.g., United States), by stage of economic development (e.g., emerging markets), by capitalization (e.g., small cap), by index (e.g., S&P 500 or Russell 1000), and by benchmark construction (e.g., equal weighted instead of cap weighted). For international investments, currency hedging is also a consideration when precisely defining the opportunity set. Asset-class returns may be accessed through public markets (e.g., listed equity) or through private markets (e.g., private equity), which introduces the question of liquidity. Sometimes, investors group assets according to a defining characteristic. For example, growth assets are usually return seeking, defensive assets are commonly thought of as risk reducing, and alternative investments are considered to be diversifying because they access relatively uncorrelated (alternative) risk premiums. We reiterate that we are not seeking to force our views regarding asset classes onto others.

We explore asset-class issues at a high level to highlight the diversity of practice. Index-fund investors typically have a relatively simple opportunity set that they seek in an investment policy—cheap, widely available asset-class exposures ("betas"). Highly sophisticated investors may have highly granular investment policies that target numerous idiosyncratic investment propositions. At its root, the matter of eligible asset classes or investments is about how *best* to capture returns, which we discuss in detail in Chapter 6.

When making selections, the fiduciary board should consider the following points about the eligible asset classes:

- *Consistency with investment beliefs*—Sometimes an investment belief has precise implications for the opportunity set. For example, a governing body may take the view that because of the nature of the investment challenge (e.g., a short-term time horizon), ready liquidity is required of all investments. We would be surprised to see a board holding such an investment belief consider private equity to be an eligible asset class. As noted in Chapter 2, in agreeing on investment beliefs, the board must consider their implications because any inconsistency between beliefs and actions leaves the governing body open to criticism.

- *Governance budget*—Some asset-class exposures should only be taken on by organizations that have the governance budget to properly judge the investment proposition, monitor its ongoing management (internally or externally), and evaluate performance. In this regard, the concept of a governance budget features (at least) two aspects: (1) the capacity required to fulfill the governance role and (2) the willingness to fulfill it. Events like the Bernie Madoff investment scandal reveal how governance mis-adventures occur again and again (see Chilton 2011). Even if a Madoff investor had the capacity to understand the type of investment strategy Madoff purported to operate—a split-strike conversion—that strategy was not actually being used. Madoff was running a Ponzi scheme, with no funds invested. Even a sophisticated investor would have had to have both the ability and willingness to discern whether Madoff was actu-ally pursuing a split-strike conversion strategy or doing something else. Clearly, many investors were not willing to carry out this part of their governance role. Instead, they relied on Madoff's reputation and track record for assurance.

- *Approval processes*—New asset classes are constantly appearing on the scene.[52] The appetite for investing in new asset classes is a function of several factors, including investment beliefs, the governance budget, and the strategic settings of the organization itself (e.g., Are we leaders? Or are we fast followers?). To the extent that the organization has an appetite to consider new asset classes eligible, we recommend that fiduciary bodies have a documented process for approving such new asset classes.[53]

In the end, the investment policy must outline the list of *eligible* asset classes or investments because doing so sends a clear signal to management

---

[52]The debate about what constitutes an asset class is ongoing and, at times, heated. We could write a separate book on the topic and still not resolve the debate. The literature on risk fac-tors has brought new focus to this debate because it seeks to reduce asset classes to underlying risk factors, some of which cut across asset classes. We return to these topics in Chapter 6.

[53]For example, at a relatively simple, modestly sized foundation, the set of eligible asset classes might be fixed and the adoption of new asset classes rare. A large, complex pension fund may consider new asset classes regularly according to a documented process. We know inves-tors who adopt a gate-based approach to new asset classes, in which investment committee approval is required for an idea to proceed through each gate. Once through the approval process, the new asset class is allowed an "incubator allocation" (say, less than a 1% allocation of the overall fund level), which allows the investor to become familiar with the investment proposition before committing (or not) to more significant allocations.

about what is the permissible opportunity set. It also serves as an important risk control.[54]

Once the opportunity set has been agreed upon, it is necessary to produce inputs (sometimes called capital market expectations) for use in the investment policy development process. In practice these inputs can be generated internally by an investment team or acquired through asset consultants and/or information providers.[55] We have observed a variety of practices in this regard.

An internal investment staff might generate assumptions by synthesizing multiple views (e.g., from consultants, investment managers, consensus estimates). At the more complex end, a substantial internal investment team with a complete research capability might be able to add value by managing assets internally using proprietary models. If that is the case, fiduciaries may need to assess the trade-off between an expensive internal capability (with known costs) running a proprietary process (with, it is hoped, well-managed risks) and the uncertain future benefits of taking such an approach.

For example, the inputs our model requires are expected returns and volatilities for each of n asset classes, skewness and kurtosis either by asset class or asset class grouping (i.e., growth vs. defensive), an $n \times n$ correlation matrix, and any asset-class restrictions, such as minimum and maximum allocations.[56] Ultimately, the precise set of inputs for a given organization will be very much a function of the organization's process. It is our view that a fiduciary should, as a minimum, develop an understanding of

- the high-level nature of the process and its inputs (e.g., Exhibit 10 and some further detail), and

- some intuition about the views being expressed through the prevailing set of inputs.

We are not saying that the governing body needs to be able to give a detailed account, such as a chief investment officer (CIO) might. We are

[54]To the extent that portfolios are implemented through delegated investment managers, the mandates for such managers must be documented so that eligible asset classes and investments are consistent with those expressed in the higher-level investment policy. In practice, subordinate mandates are merely a more granular version (say, at the security level) of mandates in the investment policy (typically, at the asset-class or sub-asset-class level).
[55]We acknowledge Shane McGarry, CFA, for his contribution to our thinking on this point.
[56]Constraints, like minimum and maximum allocations, ought to be aligned with the governance settings of the organization. Narrow ranges usually imply tighter control and less delegation to management to manage the portfolio, whereas wide ranges (especially for riskier asset classes like equities) usually imply more delegated management and a greater degree of trust in management on the part of fiduciaries.

suggesting that the governing body be diligent in its oversight of *the process.* This diligence might be as simple as having the CIO (or the most senior investment resource, internal or external) justify her or his inputs. Because good process is about *demonstrating* diligence on the part of the fiduciary, documenting and keeping records about such inquiries of management is critical.

Step 2: Portfolio Selection. Armed with the agreed-on inputs from Step 1, the analyst can model potential asset allocations for inclusion in the investment policy. As noted, we have a preference for using multiple techniques when estimating asset allocations because doing so helps us build intuition about what is optimal for a set of inputs. Looking at unconstrained portfolios—that is, ignoring minimum and maximum allocations to each asset class that was specified in Step 1—gives a sense of the impact of constraints.

The purpose of the investment policy development process is to determine the asset allocation that best addresses the HIO criteria in Step 5. But having only estimated first-pass asset allocations, one cannot understand what performance might look like beyond expected portfolio return and risk. As we emphasize in this study, we believe time-weighted returns by themselves are inadequate as a measure of performance, especially when considering retirement investing.[57] To understand what future performance *might* look like, we (1) *simulate returns* (see Step 3, Exhibit 10) and then (2) *analyze expected performance* (see Step 4, Exhibit 10).

Once we have completed Steps 2–4, we have finished the first iteration of the process aimed at finding the optimal investment solution. This process could be repeated several times for one or more reasons, such as the following:

- to explore alternatives aimed at improving expected outcomes, such as what happens if we increase the maximum allowable allocation to stocks;

- to consider marginal analysis—for example, what is the marginal impact of introducing a new asset class; or

- to conduct scenario testing, such as what happens to expected outcomes if, as some research suggests, the equity risk premium is going to be materially lower in the future than in the past.

The loop within this process may be repeated as many times as is required for the governing body to be satisfied that the investment objectives in the

---

[57]See Bianchi, Drew, and Walk (2013); Bianchi, Drew, Evans, and Walk (2014); and Drew, Stoltz, Walk, and West (2014).

HIO are being traded off optimally. Furthermore, the HIO should *always* be the touchstone for any changes to the investment portfolio.

When management comes to fiduciaries with their Next Big Idea, we recommend that fiduciaries respond with the question: How does this improve expected HIO performance? If management cannot answer the question *in terms of the HIO*, then the idea is not such a great one or the investment objectives have not sufficiently entered the managers' consciousness.

Step 3: Simulations. Before we consider the HIO, we will briefly review how we approach Steps 3 and 4, because the process outlined in this book is merely one way of developing investment policy. The details of our process may be of limited interest to readers with a different approach to investment policy development. If we hope to achieve anything it is to stimulate the interested fiduciary to get to know the processes they govern so as to become a more effective fiduciary for the benefit of beneficiaries.

With the inputs and results from previous steps, we can simulate each portfolio selection technique for a specified number of trials over a specified time horizon. For example, in practice, we might use four different simulation methods to model seven portfolio techniques over a horizon of 20 years, thus generating 10,000 synthetic return paths. Because this output is impossibly complicated, we need *effective* visualization to summarize the results. In this way, we will be able to compare the investment journey offered by each of the "optimal" strategies. When we view these strategies through the lens of the HIO, the strategy that optimally trades off the investment objectives comes into focus.

Step 4: Fiduciary Analytics. With the simulated return paths from Step 3, we are in a position to generate wealth paths by applying returns to other variables, such as current account balance (technically, wealth at time t, w_t) and contribution rates. With return paths and wealth paths, we can measure and illustrate performance in a variety of ways, such as time- and money-weighted measures, distributional properties, risk-adjusted performance measures, downside risk metrics, and visualization. We use this battery of analytics to create a three-dimensional view of expected performance in order to work through the trade-offs captured in the HIO. As the reader will see in Chapter 9, we also use these fiduciary analytics as standard when evaluating historical investment performance.

Step 5: Hierarchy of Investment Objectives. To give the reader a sense of what a HIO is and how it can be used, we reproduce one such hierarchy in **Exhibit 12**. This example includes seven prioritized investment

Exhibit 12.   Example of a Hierarchy of Investment Objectives

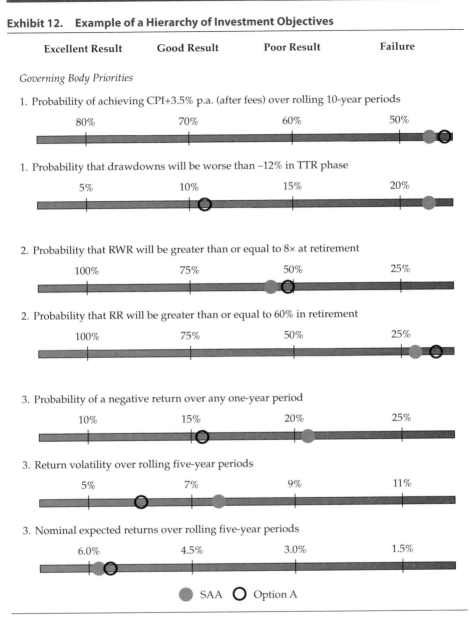

Notes: CPI is the consumer price index; SAA is strategic asset allocation.

A. Assumes long-term inflation rate of 2.5%.

B. Assumes transition to retirement (TTR) commences at 55 years of age.

C. Assumes member with a starting balance of US$250,000 at age 45, salary of US$85,000 a year, contribution rate of 10% a year, and salary growth rate of 3.0% a year. The retirement wealth ratio (RWR) compares the final accumulated balance with the assumed final-year salary of US$153,519.

D. The replacement rate (RR) is the estimated equivalent annual annuity (EAA) value for 25 years (for a life expectancy of 90 years of age) and an interest rate of 3.5%.

objectives (priorities numbered at left) and qualitative categories to allow for assessment of results from "excellent result" to "failure."

In the HIO shown in Exhibit 12, two competing investment policies are compared—the strategic asset allocation (SAA), which is the prevailing default option for a defined-contribution (DC) plan, and Option A, which is an alternative that is being considered. The reader will note the following in examining this illustrative HIO:

- Each alternative has similar performance from the perspective of return, or wealth outcomes, although in each case SAA performs marginally better.

- From a risk perspective, the differences between the two are clearer, with "Option A" being the preferred alternative.

- As expected, an obvious trade-off exists between the two alternatives. In this simple example, the fiduciary must decide between targeting a marginally better return and wealth outcome that assumes more risk or accepting a more modest outcome that assumes less risk.

Steps 6 and 7: Asset Allocation and Expectations. Once the governing body has determined which alternative offers the best strategy, it would then (1) approve and promulgate the selected asset allocation, as in Step 6, Exhibit 10; and (2) communicate the expected performance to stakeholders, as in Step 7, Exhibit 10.

These final steps must not be overlooked. Approving and formally promulgating the investment policy makes it the official investment approach of the organization. In Chapter 5, we consider in greater depth why clear and comprehensive documentation of the investment policy, in the form of an investment policy statement, is so crucial.

The final step (Step 7) is an acknowledgment that investment governance serves the broad objectives of the fiduciary investor, be that a DC plan, a defined-benefit (DB) plan, an endowment, or a foundation. For example, DC plan providers will probably have a product management group that manages the relationship between the DC plan and the plan member as a user of a product. Communication between the plan and plan member usually includes framing expectations about what the product might be expected to achieve in terms of investment performance. Some plan members may have good reason to want to know this information. For example, their financial advisers may wish to incorporate the expected return and risk of the plan member's retirement plan into a comprehensive financial plan. Whatever the reason, the "expectations" referred to in Step 7, Exhibit 10, ought to be based on the approved and promulgated investment policy of the DC plan that records what the governing body has approved, what management has implemented, and what the plan member ought to expect.

In their own words ...

"I am concerned that the overwhelming aim of most funds might really be to achieve a higher raw investment return than peers. This is left unsaid whilst we all pretend to manage to a CPI+ benchmark. As a result, investment managers find themselves without mission clarity and torn between the competing aims of members' best interests and managing peer risk."

—Michael Block

Other Ways to Think about the Issue

In the preceding HIO example, we used a single pool of assets for which a simple investment policy is being developed. In practice, there are many other ways to think about the investment problem that typically lean on the behavioral literature, especially that relating to mental accounting (Thaler 1980). Dividing the portfolio into two or more pools not only is an intuitive way of achieving multiple objectives but also avoids the situation in which the beneficiary asks too much of one portfolio, such as switching between maximizing return and minimizing risk depending on market conditions.

For example, we have used what might be described as a "two bucket" approach (see Badaoui, Deguest, Martellini, and Milhau 2014), in which we view the portfolio as having two distinct pools of assets with separate and distinct sets of objectives:

- *Liability hedging portfolio* (LHP). This kind of portfolio is a type of "safety-first" portfolio designed to maximize the probability of meeting the beneficiary's liabilities (or commitments) when they fall due (Waring 2011; Rengifo, Trendafilov, and Trifan 2014). The LHP represents the responsible risk-minimizing part of the beneficiary's investment instincts. Its investment policy seeks to hedge liabilities to a high level of probability—or to minimize the probability of "ruin" (Telser 1955).[58]

---

[58]"Ruin" in this context means the permanent inability to finance liabilities, not losing all capital, which would be its normal interpretation.

Generally speaking, the greater the certainty of return that is required, the greater the capital that needs to be committed to the LHP. In our experience, the only types of investor that can legitimately aspire to fully hedging all future liabilities are fully funded (or over-funded) DB plans and ultra-high-net-worth investors.

- *Performance-seeking portfolio* (PSP). Once (or rather if) the beneficiary's liabilities have been financed, the remaining capital can be dedicated to maximizing performance. It is available to do so because the beneficiary (theoretically) "does not need the capital." So, the ramifications of risk events are not as damaging, and their timeframe is (arguably) perpetual. This type of portfolio also appeals to the risk-seeking instincts of some investors (e.g., entrepreneurs, some of whom are the same ultra-high-net-worth investors able to successfully use such an approach). A risk we have observed is that if the PSP performs well, the investor inevitably wants to adopt the PSP investment strategy for LHP capital. In such situations, the counsel of the adviser or consultant can *remind* the beneficiary of the distinct purposes (and objectives) of the LHP and PSP.

Obviously, available capital can be divided in many other ways into conceptual "pools," and an investment policy can be established for each pool. In creating pools, we believe the following points are key:

- Whatever the number of pools, the process outlined in this chapter can serve as a blueprint for how each portfolio's investment policy can be developed.

- The overall investment policy—that is, the weighted sum of the investment policies of the individual pools—should be checked to ensure that it fits with the overall levels of risk the fiduciary board has in mind for the beneficiary.

- The fiduciaries must press management (and any asset consultants) to make the case that the additional complexity of having multiple pools, sets of investment objectives, and investment policies, and so on, will be rewarded with superior outcomes. As the global financial crisis of 2007–2008 showed us vividly, in matters of investment, complexity is not free.

Myriad Issues to Consider

With portfolio selection there are myriad settings that will, or may, influence investment policy that aren't addressed specifically in this book because the details—as opposed to the high-level settings—are more than a fiduciary would be reasonably required to understand:

- whether the portfolio has a static or dynamic asset allocation;

- income and liquidity requirements;

- frictions—the impact of fees, taxes, and turnover and how these aspects are managed and controlled in capturing returns;

- policies toward hedging, rebalancing, and so on; and

- risk management considerations, both in an investment sense and in terms of the broader organizational risk context.

Most of these policies are related to how returns are captured. We discuss these issues at length in Chapter 6.

In ending this chapter, we leave the final word on portfolio choice to Ben Bernanke, former chairman of the US Federal Reserve: "Economic engineering is about the design and analysis of frameworks for achieving specific economic objectives" (Bernanke 2010). Portfolio choice is essentially an economic engineering task that uses portfolio selection principles and techniques to solve the problem of "optimally" trading off competing investment objectives.[59]

Points for Reflection: Chapter 4. Portfolio Choice: Getting to the Destination

As a fiduciary:

- Can I explain how the specification of the investment challenge—that is, the critical investment objectives in order of priority—results in an "optimal" asset allocation?

- Do I have confidence that the investment process is defensible, repeatable, and documented?

- Do I understand how the organization defines the investment opportunity set (eligible asset classes), and is the opportunity set consistent with the organization's investment beliefs and philosophy?

---

[59]Before our friends in the hard sciences take exception, we are not implying that said principles, and related techniques, are as mathematically certain as some that physical scientists deal with. We would argue that if there is an analogy to the sciences it might be medicine. Like medicine, we don't always understand the underlying process, but we can observe symptoms upon which to base diagnosis and treatment.

- Am I aware of the kinds of assumptions that underlie the investment process and how they are determined and approved?

- Can I comfortably say that the investment portfolio is the best way to achieve the investment objectives of our beneficiaries?

- Can I say that when we reconsider the investment strategy, we evaluate proposed changes in light of the marginal benefit/cost in achieving the HIO?

- Am I comfortable that those parts of the organization that need to know about the outcomes of the investment policy development process do know?

- Do asset consultants play a significant part in the investment policy development process? Do I understand how they generate their contribution?

- Does the investment policy development process reasonably balance simplicity and complexity?

5. The Investment Policy Statement: Publishing the Battle Plan

"No battle plan survives contact with the enemy."

—*Helmuth von Moltke, the Elder ([1871] 1971)*[60]

In this chapter, we conclude Step P in the *OPERIS* framework, as shown in **Exhibit 13**, by documenting the essential elements of the investment policy approved by the governing body in the form of an investment policy statement (IPS). The aim of the stated IPS is to give all stakeholders a *common understanding* of how fiduciaries plan to "solve" the beneficiary's investment problem.

Opening a chapter that emphasizes the importance of documenting the investment policy with a quote like von Moltke's may seem strange. If an investment policy, like a battle plan, is not much use when it meets reality,

Exhibit 13. *OPERIS* Framework: Policy, Part 2

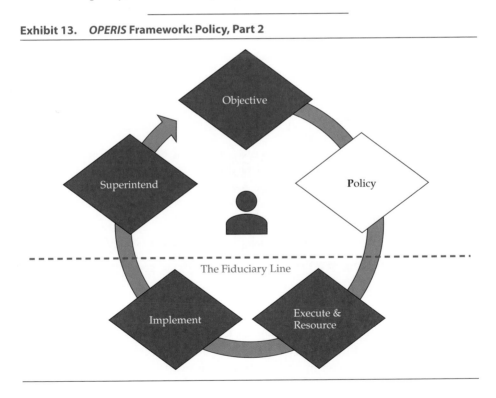

[60]Helmuth von Moltke, the Elder (1800–1891), was a German/Prussian general and military strategist.

then why bother? We think that Dwight D. Eisenhower, 34th president of the United States and former five-star general, had the answer when he stated, "Plans are worthless, but *planning* is *everything*"[61] [emphasis added].

With this statement we most certainly agree. A documented investment policy may look less than advisable in light of prevailing market conditions, but it still represents the *planning* undertaken by the governing body on the part of beneficiaries to address the underlying investment challenge. As we have noted, the planning, and subsequent decision making, is conducted in a context of uncertainty.

Does a documented investment policy not then have the advantage of recording the *substance* of the investment decisions made to achieve the investment objectives contained in the hierarchy of investment objectives (HIO)? Surely, such an investment policy at least results in a common understanding about how best to proceed to achieve the investment objectives of beneficiaries in volatile market conditions. We address these assumptions in two parts:

- Yes, we agree that creating a common understanding about the substance of the governing body's decisions is desirable.

- No, we do not believe that this common understanding always happens in practice.

In their own words ...

"Carefully considering the true objective for the plan and measuring success relative to that objective is critical to success as well as to guarding against the risk of ruin. Defined-contribution plans generally should be judged based on how well they are meeting or are likely to meet the worker's need for retirement income."

—*Stacy Schaus, Founder and CEO, Schaus Group LLC*

War Stories from the Field

To make our point, we share two anecdotes. The first comes from a consulting engagement we conducted with an institutional investor, and the second, an experience as a member of an investment committee.

---

[61]Dwight D. Eisenhower, *Public Papers of the Presidents of the United States* (Washington, DC: Federal Register Division, 1957): 818.

Consulting Engagement. We were engaged by a foundation to test its prevailing investment policy in light of the objectives outlined in its documented IPS.[62] At the outset, we asked the internal investment staff to provide us with the IPS and other relevant documentation. By interpreting what we read, and with no other input, we listed and prioritized what we thought the investor's investment objectives were. We then asked the internal investment staff and the investment committee (the delegate of the board of directors on investment matters) what they thought the foundation's investment objectives were and in what order of priority.

What did we find?

Somewhat surprisingly, each of the three parties had different objectives *and* different priorities. The list of objectives we generated had five objectives ranked in order of importance from most important (1) to least important (5). The final, moderated list of objectives, using the same numbers for the items in the list, was 3 (most important), then 2, and then 1 (least important). Our objectives 4 and 5 were not even considered important enough to be objectives. Our different readings of the IPS not only resulted in different sets of objectives in different priorities but also revealed a difference in emphasis. Our set of objectives prioritized return over risk, whereas the client's priorities showed that risk management was more decisive than return generation.

For us the experience was instructive. Without a shared mission—or a common destination, to use the aviation metaphor—solving the beneficiary's investment challenge is fraught at best. It is for this reason that we provided a chapter on documenting the investment policy (we return to this issue in Chapter 8).

Investment Committee Experience. The second anecdote is related to membership of the investment committee of a charity. By way of context, the governance arrangements of the broader charitable group were what might be described as complex, with governance responsibilities shared among multiple bodies.

In particular, the main governing body—to which the aforementioned investment committee was accountable on investment matters—had broad responsibilities and consisted mainly of volunteers. This circumstance created a desire for efficiency so as to spend the limited governance budget wisely. Efficiency was such a priority that the governing body called for a revision of the IPS from a modest length to an even more modest length. What was already a relatively short IPS became shorter still.

---

[62]As with many investors, the client wondered whether its inflation-linked investment objective was achievable in the context of the modest returns expected from most asset classes. For a discussion on the "mystery" of low and negative interest rates, see Siegel and Sexauer (2017).

Although the IPS might have been becoming too short, this exercise was not the real problem. According to our diagnosis, the investment committee had at least two serious problems:

1. *Content.* In shortening the IPS, the secretary to the investment committee had changed the IPS in substance as well as form, thus undermining the original intent.

2. *Role clarity.* The most substantial (proposed) change was the role of the investment committee itself. According to the "long" (original) IPS, that role was relatively broad: to provide advice and make recommendations on investment policies. According to the condensed IPS, the role was qualitatively different and more narrowly defined, namely, the committee was tasked with the oversight of management and the provision of advice on the implementation of the IPS.

We thus see the second-order impacts of the pressures facing the governing body. In an effort to shorten and simplify the IPS, the investment governance apparatus called into question elements of the IPS and, arguably, undermined the IPS as a "source of truth" regarding investment *planning*. This resulted in an investment policy that was less clear and had more ambiguous roles and responsibilities than the original.

This example also underlines our point that the governance budget should be aligned with the prevailing governance arrangements. With relatively complex arrangements, involving multiple bodies with overlapping (investment and noninvestment) responsibilities, the governance budget ought to be relatively significant. Unfortunately, given its nature as a charity, this organization's governing bodies consisted of volunteers (or those providing *pro bono* services), which introduced the opposite pressure on the governance budget—that is, one of minimizing it.

We have told this story not as a gratuitous critique of the particular charity. All the individuals were acting professionally and inspired by the right motives. Rather, this example reveals the reality that most fiduciary investors face. The real world of investing on behalf of others is a great deal more complex—involving uncomfortable trade-offs—than a standard investment textbook would have one believe. The challenge becomes an exercise in dealing with the facts *as they are* and (hopefully!) making sensible decisions that are based on a defensible, repeatable, and documented process, such as *OPERIS*.

In their own words …

"Investment governance is one of the strongest levers that enables super-annuation fund trustees to deliver the best retirement outcomes for their members. It matters because those that actually do the investing cannot also perform a true governance function."

—*Pauline Vamos, former CEO, Regnan, and*
independent non-executive director,
Mercer Superannuation (Australia) Limited

Universal Principles

This book is not about mandating a worldview (as if that were possible). We seek to present universal principles that, if applied faithfully, will serve all fiduciaries.

When it comes to documenting an investment policy there are usually sufficient differences between fiduciary investors, where the task is a function of the beneficiary and the investment problem. Put another way, when it comes to drafting an IPS there are dangers to industrialization. Therefore, in developing an IPS, the following principles (summarized in **Exhibit 14**) are helpful:

- *Comparative advantages.* Fiduciary investors usually have one or more comparative advantages in investing. For example, defined-contribution (DC) plans usually have long investment horizons, and endowments usually have relatively certain commitments year to year. We would be surprised if an IPS did not record such comparative advantages (to the extent they exist), and use them as the motivation for the actual investment approach contained in the IPS.

- *Alignment.* The IPS should demonstrate that there is alignment throughout the investment policy. For example, the IPS should record the governing body's investment beliefs and then enumerate an investment policy that *aligns* with those beliefs.

- *Clarity.* As our anecdotes demonstrate, clarity is an important principle when documenting the investment policy. First, an IPS should be written in plain language. In addition (as shown in the first anecdote), *clarity*

Exhibit 14. Principles for Documenting an Investment Policy Statement

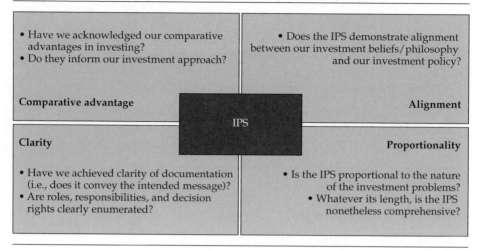

- Have we acknowledged our comparative advantages in investing?
- Do they inform our investment approach?

Comparative advantage

- Does the IPS demonstrate alignment between our investment beliefs/philosophy and our investment policy?

Alignment

IPS

Clarity

Proportionality

- Have we achieved clarity of documentation (i.e., does it convey the intended message)?
- Are roles, responsibilities, and decision rights clearly enumerated?

- Is the IPS proportional to the nature of the investment problems?
- Whatever its length, is the IPS nonetheless comprehensive?

of documentation is required; that is, the written IPS should faithfully recount the *substance* of the investment decisions made by the governing body. Moreover (as the second anecdote highlights), the *roles, responsibilities, and rights* of the bodies and individuals need to be clear. The IPS should clearly state which parties bear what responsibilities.

- *Proportionality.* The IPS ought to be proportional to the nature of the investment challenge. Relatively simple investment issues can be addressed with a brief IPS; complex investment problems may need to be much longer to reasonably document how the governing body sets out to achieve the investment objectives on behalf of beneficiaries. For example, as of April 2017, the California Public Employees' Retirement System had a "total fund investment policy" that was 98 pages long (CalPERS 2017).[63] We are aware of IPS for ultra-high-net-worth (UHNW) individuals that have separate and distinct investment strategies for the numerous entities involved (e.g., the UHNW individual, the spouse, one or more investment trusts, a foundation).

Some of these themes will be revisited in later chapters as we investigate steps below the fiduciary line.

---

[63]CalPERS is the pension scheme for public employees of the State of California. As of 30 June 2016, it had 1.8 million members representing 3,021 employers and $302 billion in funds under management (CalPERS 2016).

We do not intend to provide a *pro forma* IPS for the reader's consideration, but the following list provides a start as to the sections or headings the IPS should contain:

- *Context*—Important background should be discussed in a section to provide context for the remainder of the document. This background might include higher-level financial objectives within which the investment objectives exist (see Chapter 3).

- *Investment beliefs*—The outline of the investment beliefs should be included as suggested in Chapter 2.

- *Roles, responsibilities, and delegations*—A section should identify all of the stakeholders and specify who has the right to make what decisions; the approval and oversight processes should be explained (see Chapter 3).

- *Investment purpose*—A section should provide a qualitative description of the purpose of the pool of assets. This section might include a discussion of entities and structures, sources and uses of funds, cash flow requirements, and risk preferences (see Chapter 3).

- *Strategy toward environmental, social, and governance (ESG) factors*—If the governing body has investment beliefs relating to ESG factors in investing (see Chapter 2), this information should be spelled out. Detail may need to be documented to outline how these beliefs are to be reflected in the investment portfolio.

- *Investment objectives*—The document should provide, from the perspective of the *OPERIS* framework, a list of all investment objectives, in order of priority, in the form of an HIO for each pool of assets (see Chapters 3 and 4). Such objectives are likely to include one or more risk-related criteria, in which risk is measured in a way that is consistent with the risk preferences of the governing body.

- *Asset allocation strategy*—For each distinct pool of assets, documentation of the investment strategy should be stated in terms that are consistent with the approved opportunity set (see Chapter 4). The opportunity set—the asset classes and sub-asset-classes eligible for investment—can be outlined in separate sections or as an appendix to the IPS (to allow for change without the need to formally amend the whole IPS).

- *Benchmarks*—The benchmarks that represent each asset or sub-asset-class in the approved opportunity set (see Chapter 6) should be spelled out.

- *Due diligence requirements*—The due diligence requirements for all investments (be they securities, funds, limited partnerships, or assets) and investment managers (see Chapter 7) should be stated.

- *Monitoring and reporting requirements*—The document should identify the monitoring and reporting requirements necessary for the governing body and/or its delegates to exercise oversight over the investment portfolio and all parties to whom tasks are delegated (see Chapters 8 and 9).

- *Risk management*—Sections should deal with all relevant risk management considerations, such as investment risk management, derivatives and counterparty risk, and so on. Drafting such requirements in conjunction with the risk management and compliance functions of the investment organization is advisable to ensure alignment with broader internal requirements as well as legislative and regulatory requirements (see Chapters 8 and 9).

- *Custody*—A separate section should outline how safe custody of investments is ensured (see Chapter 8).

- *Other issues*—Details regarding accounting for fees and expenses, liquidity, rebalancing, hedging, leverage, securities lending, and so on (see Chapter 7) should be stated.

Other sections may be important to specific investment committees. They would depend on the nature of the beneficiary or the investment challenge. For example, tax matters are likely to be more important for UHNW individuals than for, say, a tax-exempt government defined-benefit plan.[64]

We end this chapter by returning to another aspect of Herr von Moltke's strategic thought: "Strategy is a system of expedients." The process of planning that results in an investment policy, if effective and clearly communicated, can assist fiduciaries, and those that act on their behalf, to expediently deal with what financial markets throw at them to the benefit of beneficiaries.

---

[64]For further guidance on IPS construction, see Boone and Lubitz (2004), DiBruno (2013), and fi360 (2016).

Points for Reflection: Chapter 5. The Investment Policy Statement: Publishing the Battle Plan

As a fiduciary:

- Could I present a copy of my organization's current IPS if requested?

- Am I satisfied that the IPS represents a common understanding— among fiduciaries, management, consultants, and so on—of the HIO and how they are to be achieved?

- Am I comfortable that our organization's IPS is consistent with the universal principles suggested in this chapter—namely, comparative advantages, alignment, clarity, and proportionality?

- Can I say that our organization's IPS contains all necessary information?

6. Below the Fiduciary Line: "The Doing"

"We need a mutual fund industry with both vision and values; a vision of *fiduciary duty* and shareholder service and values rooted in the proven principles of long-term investing and of *trusteeship* that demands integrity in *serving our clients*."

—*John C. Bogle*[65]

In the previous four chapters, we were concerned with beliefs (Chapter 2), investment objectives (Chapter 3), portfolio choice (Chapter 4), and the investment policy statement (IPS; Chapter 5). These are all important considerations *above* the fiduciary line in *OPERIS*. We now enter Step E&R of the framework—that is, **E**xecute and **R**esource (see **Exhibit 15**).

Exhibit 15. *OPERIS* Framework: Execute & Resource

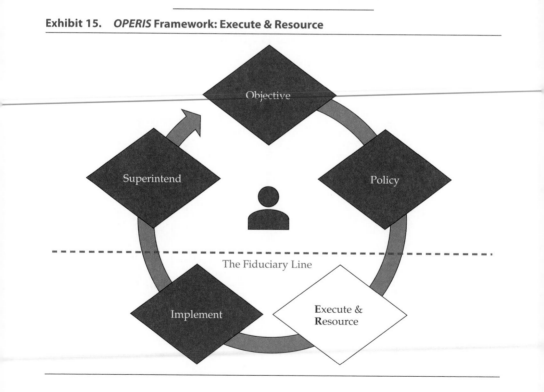

[65]John C. Bogle (1929–2019) was the founder of the Vanguard Group. Quote is from John C. Bogle, "Designing a New Mutual Fund Industry," Bogle Financial Markets Research Center (20 February 2007): www.vanguard.com/bogle_site/sp20070220.htm.

We have reached the point in the investment process at which the fiduciary typically has less visibility, and more work and responsibility are delegated to others. These delegations must be understood. As we move to Step E&R, opacity is increasing. The challenge before the governing body on matters below the fiduciary line is to ensure the alignment of this and Step I (Implement) with the settings above the line, in the presence of heightened opacity.

The issues discussed in the previous chapters still apply, with the most important being that *fiduciaries cannot delegate accountability.*[66] As we will discuss, although agents are both important and useful in fulfilling some of the roles required to be undertaken in both Step E&R and Step I, accountability ultimately rests with the fiduciary.

In the *OPERIS* framework, activities below the fiduciary line may be thought of as the "doing" steps—where the rubber meets the road. Strategy formulation has ended, and investment policy *implementation* has begun. Below the fiduciary line is also, on many occasions, where the trouble starts. Most important for the beneficiary, alignment is sorely tested.

Given the increased opacity of what is going on below the fiduciary line, all those who serve the fiduciary investor, above and below the line, must have clear roles and responsibilities—that is, decision rights. **Exhibit 16** provides an example from a pension fund of how this information can be spelled out.

While reading this chapter, keep in mind the origins of the theme that underpins this book: Governance is a way of fulfilling a fiduciary duty. *Executing* good governance ensures compliance and promotes a culture of beneficiary-centric decision making across the investment organization. We explore the practicalities of *resourcing* "the doing" and discuss the importance of the governing body concentrating its scarce governance resources on high-value-added activities. Finally, much of this chapter is dedicated to how the governing body executes and resources its policy to capture returns in light of its beliefs (Chapter 2).

In the following consideration of some of the issues fiduciary investors face in *executing* and *resourcing* the agreed strategy, we do not claim that the discussion is comprehensive. We illuminate some of the challenges facing the governing body when going below the fiduciary line. As history has taught us, any fortress—military or metaphorical—is only as strong as its weakest link.

---

[66]Fiduciaries cannot delegate accountability for their duties to beneficiaries (Bailey and Richards 2017). They can, however, share responsibility with delegates. In this chapter and Chapter 7, we delve into what might be required to share this responsibility and provide oversight in an effective way.

Exhibit 16.   Example of Delegation and Clarity of Decision Rights: New Zealand Super Fund

Who Makes Investment Decisions?	
Who	What Decisions
Board	• Sets investment policy for the Fund
	• Decides on an appropriate total level of risk for the Fund
	• Approves and monitors investment strategies
	• Appoints the Fund's Custodian (a custodian holds all of the Fund's listed assets and provides investment administration services)
	• Approves new investment managers (where there is an Investment Management Agreement)
Management	• Provides investment policy advice to the Board
	• Decides how to allocate total Fund risk between baskets of assets with similar characteristics, and then within each basket
	• Implements agreed investment strategies and identifies investment opportunities
	• Monitors and reports on the performance of investment strategies and of the Fund as a whole
	• Monitors the ongoing suitability of appointed investment managers
Appointed external investment managers	• Make investment choices on behalf of the Guardians, subject to an Investment
	• Management agreement or the terms of a collective investment vehicle

Source: Guardians of the New Zealand Super Fund (2017).

We will show that the effective fiduciary executes and resources a defensible, repeatable, and documented investment process to protect the beneficiary.

Executing Good Governance

In Chapter 1, we said that investment governance referred to the effective use of resources—people, policies, processes, and systems—by an individual or governing body (the fiduciary or agent) to fulfill a fiduciary duty. We emphasize the importance of "effective use" and the challenges facing the governing body to execute and resource good investment governance. Faced with the specter of reduced transparency in governing Step E&R in the *OPERIS* framework, it is timely to revisit the formal link between the enduring principles of good governance and fiduciary duty.

In their own words ...

"[T]he pillars of a strong investment governance program are transparency, independence, and diversity of input and oversight. Governance and decision making should ultimately be focused on ensuring a plan participant's financial security."

—David Skinner, Executive Director, PGIM Real Estate

Unlike the etymology of the word governance—which has Greek origins, *to steer* (see Scharfman 2015)—fiduciary comes from the Latin *fiducia*, meaning to trust.[67] A fiduciary is one who is trusted. In the presence of opacity and increasing complexity, however, fiduciaries are called upon to place their trust in others (say, external investment managers). They must share responsibility as they steer the investment organization toward achieving the beneficiary's objectives. This sharing introduces the idea that in the execution of governance, more than one trust relationship is present. As we discussed in Chapter 1, the classical relationship is that between the beneficiary and the fiduciary. Only in the simplest of cases, however, does it end there. In practice, the fiduciary trusts others to act according to the delegations agreed to by the fiduciary to facilitate the execution and implementation of the IPS (Chapter 5). In this context, a metaphorical chain of trusting relationships exists, as shown in **Exhibit 17**.[68]

As noted in Chapter 1, the specific legal definition (and obligations) of fiduciaries (incorporating their chain of trusting relationships) varies between jurisdictions and investor types (in our three contexts: defined-contribution [DC] plans, defined-benefit [DB] plans, and endowments and foundations

---

[67]Rahaim (2005) explained that, "in its basic meaning, a fiduciary is a person charged by law and equity with a higher duty to care for another person. Developing from Latin, the word *fiducia* means 'trust' and carries connotations of total trust, good faith and honesty. Fiduciary may be defined as to be in trust, in confidence." The word "fiduciary" may trace back to the third century BCE and the work of a Roman playwright, Titus Maccius Plautus. It applies to a situation in which someone (or something) has been entrusted to another (Watson 1991). This author also notes the link that fiducia has with the Roman goddess of faith, Fides.

[68]Increasingly, the media and literature reflect debate about who in the financial services industry should be held to a fiduciary standard—and the answer is not always the party who has the relationship with the principal. We think this debate is healthy for an industry that is still trying to regain the trust it had before the global financial crisis of 2007–2008.

Exhibit 17.   Links in the Chain of Trusting Relationships

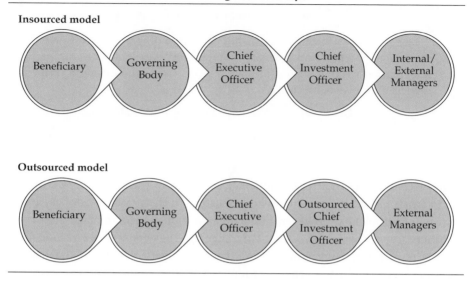

Insourced model

Beneficiary · Governing Body · Chief Executive Officer · Chief Investment Officer · Internal/External Managers

Outsourced model

Beneficiary · Governing Body · Chief Executive Officer · Outsourced Chief Investment Officer · External Managers

[E&Fs]).[69] Moreover, as noted by Rahaim (2005), the laws relating to governance and fiduciary duty are ever changing.

A fiduciary is not sismply an *agent* of a principal. Agents are obliged to carry out the wishes of a principal, whereas a fiduciary's obligation is to exercise independent judgment on behalf of a beneficiary (Bower and Paine 2017). This distinction is important. As Bower and Paine noted, "An agent is an order taker, whereas a fiduciary is expected to make discretionary decisions." Thus, fiduciary duty entails higher obligations of care; it cannot be fulfilled by simply ticking off the right boxes in the right order.

OPERIS is a continuous process that fortifies investment governance. We reject the idea that the investment governance process is "set and forget" in nature. Investment governance is a dynamic, ongoing process of continuous improvement that reflects that "anxious vigilance" (Smith [1776] 1937) expected of a fiduciary that we discussed in Chapter 1. Having a defensible, repeatable, and documented investment process may be one of the few comparative advantages a fiduciary may hold over other investors. This idea is

---

[69]Logue and Rader (1998) noted that US DC plans entail an even more stringent standard of care for fiduciaries. The Employee Retirement Income Security Act of 1974 (ERISA) requires the fiduciary to use "care, skill, prudence and diligence" and to act in the same way that someone "familiar with such matters"—in short, a "prudent expert"—would act (p. 40). The Australian Prudential Regulation Authority (APRA) requires trustees of superannuation plans to have an investment governance framework "appropriate to the size, business mix and complexity" of the regulated entity's operations (APRA 2013a).

underpinned by the work of Clark and Urwin (2008, 2010), who noted the contribution of good governance to value creation among institutional asset owners. Other research has suggested that the gains to good governance, in a return sense, might be as high as 1%–3% per annum (Watson Wyatt 2006; Ambachtsheer 2007).

We turn now to Step E&R—the execution and resourcing of the strategy, the doing.

Resourcing "the Doing"

Excellence of execution requires both appropriate resourcing and efficient and effective implementation to achieve objectives in the hierarchy of investment objectives (HIO). We begin with resourcing and the governance budget.

Unfortunately, fiduciary investors all too commonly frame resourcing as a type of insurance issue—that is, a known cost today for an uncertain future benefit. We challenge this framing throughout the chapter. Moreover, we conceptualize the governance budget for the fiduciary investor in broad terms, including time (and the focus of governance time [GT]), talent (the composition and complementarity of the skills of those who serve on the governing body and the delegates who serve them), and resourcing support for investment-related risk management (and integration with enterprise-wide systems of control). The quantity of resourcing and governance budget required should be consistent with the scale, complexity, and nature of the investment challenge the beneficiary faces (see Chapter 1).

To begin, consider time as a component of the governance budget. As a simple heuristic, consider, for your organization, the ratio of funds under management (FuM), given in dollars or the equivalent, to GT, given in hours—that is, FuM:GT.[70] For every one hour of GT, how much FuM is being governed?

A common practice is for the investment committee of a fiduciary investor to meet for, say, 2 hours, bimonthly—a not-grand sum of 12 hours a year—to govern many hundreds of millions (commonly, billions) of dollars of "other people's money." For some large DB and DC plans (and some large endowments), the FuM:GT ratio, standardized by time, is a flabbergasting sight. We encourage fiduciary investors, as an exercise, to find out for their organizations what parameters *a* through *h* are in the "resourcing envelope" (the investment governance budget) shown in **Exhibit 18**.

---

[70]Governance time is only one part of the governance budget as discussed previously, but here we are trying to draw the connection between the time spent by the governing body with the magnitude of the responsibility they discharge as proxied by FuM.

Exhibit 18.   The Resourcing Envelope

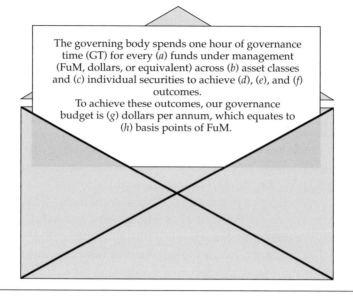

The governing body spends one hour of governance time (GT) for every (*a*) funds under management (FuM, dollars, or equivalent) across (*b*) asset classes and (*c*) individual securities to achieve (*d*), (*e*), and (*f*) outcomes.

To achieve these outcomes, our governance budget is (*g*) dollars per annum, which equates to (*h*) basis points of FuM.

When the parameters are filled in, you can consider the most important questions. Are you, as the fiduciary, comfortable that the investment organization is sufficiently resourced to execute the investment strategy and achieve the objectives consistent with a fiduciary standard of care?

At this juncture, we want the reader to understand what we are *not* saying:

- We are not suggesting that more time is necessarily better. In fact, we believe that *role clarity* is critical because delegations become increasingly important as FuM increases.[71]

- We also are not saying that throwing more money at investment governance guarantees success. We have observed, however, that many fiduciary investors are chronically underresourced from a governance perspective, particularly as they reach for return (and assume the complexity that typically comes with such a decision) in the low-expected-return world in which we currently live.[72]

---

[71]We encourage the reader to think specifically about the talent (or lack of talent) and alignment of those sitting around the fiduciary table and those who serve the board.

[72]For a survey of capital market expectations of leading investment houses, as of 7 May 2017, see Santoli (2017). See also Siegel and Sexauer (2017) on asset allocation in a low-expected-return world.

Given the magnitude of the task, we are saying that the fiduciary must be *satisfied* that the execution and implementation of the strategy are appropriately resourced. An investment process is only as strong as its weakest link, so we encourage all fiduciary investors to formally consider, on a regular basis, the link that is the governance budget in light of the complexity of the investment organization.

If GT is a scarce commodity, our observations suggest that the time dedicated to future-oriented, strategic investment decisions is even more scarce. For example, consider the investment committee agenda of the hypothetical ABC Fund as given in **Exhibit 19**. This investment committee meets six times a year for two hours per meeting. Total FuM at the ABC Fund currently stands at US$12 billion.[73]

We can begin to estimate for the ABC Fund some of the parameters in the resourcing envelope using simple calculations. This approach will shed some light on the task before the committee. First, you should know that at a recent offsite strategy session, the ABC Fund Investment Committee confirmed that shorter, more frequent (every other month) meetings would allow investment governance to be more *nimble, agile,* and *responsive* to manager selection issues and market events.

We support the idea that the investment process should not be held hostage to the rigidities of the investment committee cycle (and we encourage the use of circular resolution and other formal vote-outside-committee mechanisms, when required). It is fascinating, however, that important motivators for the investment committee at the hypothetical ABC Fund—that is, agility, nimbleness, and responsiveness—are linked with *manager selection* and *market timing*. More important, both of the agenda items related to these topics are there for *decisions* and account for *two-thirds* of the total meeting time. Why?

At the recent offsite strategy meeting of the ABC Fund, the members would have been prudent to reflect on some of the following, perhaps more difficult, questions regarding the allocation of time on the agenda:

---

[73]We have kept the mathematics simple in our example for ease of interpretation of the FuM:GT. To provide some context, at the end of 2016, the top three pension funds by FuM (US$ million) in the Pensions & Investments/Willis Towers Watson 300 ranking were the Government Pension Investment of Japan, with total assets of US$1,237,636; the Government Pension Fund of Norway, with US$893,088; and the US Federal Retirement Thrift, with US$485,575. For further details and the full listing, see Willis Towers Watson (2017b). In our hypothetical example, FuM of US$12 billion would not result in the fund being in the largest 300 pension funds in the world (number 300 is Telstra Super of Australia with US$13.3 billion).

Exhibit 19. Agenda of the Hypothetical ABC Fund

Meeting of the Investment Committee of the ABC Fund

July XX, 20XX

9:30am to 11:30am

1. Committee-Only Session: Open Agenda	[5 minutes]
2. Review and Approval of May XX, 2018 Investment Committee Minutes	[5 minutes]
3. June Quarter Performance Review (includes manager evaluation)	[15 minutes]
4. FOR DECISION: Private Real Estate Core Manager Search	
• Manager presentations:	
i. "DEF Investment Management"	[30 minutes]
ii. "XYZ Capital Investors"	[30 minutes]
5. FOR DECISION: Market Timing Position	
• Reduction in Fixed Interest Weights	[30 minutes]
6. Other Business	[5 minutes]

- Is manager selection a source of comparative advantage for the investment committee?

- Does the committee have an informational advantage or a special competence regarding manager selection in any asset class (in the example, core managers in private real estate are mentioned)?

- Is this approach to manager selection and market timing consistent with the investment beliefs of ABC Fund? If so, over what time horizon: day-to-day, week-to-week, or month-to-month?[74]

- On controversial matters, such as manager selection and market timing, are these decisions best made by the investment committee? If not, what are the appropriate resources and governance processes required to delegate these decisions?

- Most important, will undertaking these two activities at the committee level improve the probability we will achieve our investment objectives?

We are not suggesting that issues of manager selection and market timing are irrelevant and unworthy of fiduciary consideration. Quite the contrary. We are challenging whether these decisions are best made *directly* by the investment committee or by *delegating*—the sharing of responsibility—to specialized experts advising the committee. Without such role clarity, we have witnessed, first-hand, how the one hour dedicated to agenda item 4 can go by quickly when working through impressive PowerPoint presentations and chatting with smart investment professionals (with a side of coffee and freshly baked muffins, of course).

The doing must start with—and always be crafted, executed, and resourced by—the governing body—that is, those above the fiduciary line. If the governing body does not tell service providers (say, investment managers) what they are supposed to achieve (their objective, as an input to achieving the HIO), how they are to do it (the mandate), and how their performance will be monitored and rewarded (*superintending* will be discussed in Chapters 8 and 9), the fiduciary investor has, in our view, commenced the governance process *below the line*, which is the wrong place.

Governing bodies (and/or their delegates) can—unthinkingly, at times—jump above and below the fiduciary line with disconcerting ease. The cause is either ambiguous roles and responsibilities or an unwillingness to carry out the defined roles and responsibilities outlined in the IPS (see Chapter 5). Precision regarding decision rights—above and below the fiduciary line—is critical for the effective conduct of Step E&R in the *OPERIS* framework. Given that the fiduciary cannot outsource accountability, how the fiduciary investor executes and resources the investment process becomes paramount to fulfilling her or his duty to the beneficiary.

---

[74]See Bauer and Dahlquist (2001) and Drew (2006) for the forecast accuracy required for successful market timing on a monthly basis.

The Key Challenge: Accountability Cannot Be Outsourced

The fiduciary lives in a world in which accountability cannot be outsourced. Regulators seem to codify further duties for the fiduciary every day (in addition to fiduciary duty at common law in relevant jurisdictions). That oversight is not necessarily a bad thing. Capital market history is littered with tales of questionable behavior by fiduciaries toward those to whom they owed their duty. So, adherence to a defensible, repeatable, and documented investment process that *binds the fiduciary to the beneficiary* is an important step in meeting fiduciary duty.[75]

Given this context, a key issue for the fiduciary is how to understand the division of labor (roles and responsibilities) across the investment process. The distinguishable, but aligned, roles must work in concert in the best interests of beneficiaries.

Unfortunately, investment governance is an activity prone to *ambiguity*. A common understanding seems to be absent.[76] In too many instances, the location of the fiduciary line is typically known only *after* an adverse event has affected the investment organization:

- Something has apparently gone wrong.

- Accusations are made.

- Records (e.g., minutes and committee papers) are checked.

- Answers are found (or not).

The best way to bring these ideas to life is by example: The cash portfolio at the hypothetical ABC Fund has performed well for many years (i.e., has produced superior risk-adjusted returns over the agreed Treasury bill index). The mandate for the fund is broad and allows the investment manager to hold "cash and cash-like securities." The fiduciary has been happy with the portfolio's returns over cash. Unbeknown to the investment committee, however, the source of the reported alpha has been an active program of capturing the credit premium (call it "alpha lite," "beta prime," or less charitably, an

---

[75]The role of the governing body is not simply to review and approve investment strategies. The governing body needs to also satisfy itself that an effective system of risk management and internal control is established and maintained and that the organization's managers monitor the effectiveness of the risk management practices. Such a disintermediated approach to risk management reflects the "three lines of defense" paradigm, which we return to in Chapter 9.

[76]In this circumstance, an IPS can come in handy because it can record a common understanding. Done poorly, however, the IPS can both enshrine the ambiguity and record the misunderstanding.

unconscious or concealed "credit bet"). A negative credit event occurs. Purely for the purposes of illustration, let's call it a global financial crisis.

Suddenly, those above the line discover new clarity about the actual objective for the cash portfolio; that is, it needs to be a source of liquidity. This new clarity results in the investment committee demanding that the portfolio be more "cash" and less "cash-like." In this story:

- Something apparently goes wrong—a negative credit event occurred.

- Accusations are made—investment managers are summoned to the investment committee for "a meeting."

- Records (e.g., minutes and committee papers) are checked—"So much alpha; where has it all gone?" "Why is alpha so negative?" "This is not the process we wanted (*in hindsight*); we need liquidity." "This manager is not achieving the objectives we want. Let's terminate this manager and revise the mandate."

- Answers are found (or not)—"What do they mean by 'cash-like'?" "Why were we not informed that cash-like meant mortgage-backed securities?" "Who is responsible?"

Investment managers are literal.

Indeed, all those below the line are *literal*. They *literally* read "cash and cash-like" within the policy settings, and *literally* acted within the confines of that policy (as they are permitted to do) to meet the stated objectives. The easiest way to beat a cash benchmark for a "cash and cash-like" portfolio is to take more risk—for example, credit risk.[77]

Therefore, mandated documentation, service-level agreements, and investment administration are key pillars to the implementation of any strategy. How the fiduciary *superintends* those with whom they have shared responsibility (see Chapters 8 and 9)—including drafting, updating, and implementing the necessary documentation—is critical.

The parable of the "cash and cash-like" portfolio at the ABC Fund raises many issues. What is a better way for the ABC Fund investment committee to spend time—listening to manager presentations for an hour or spending an hour on *superintending* the process of manager selection? Spending 30 minutes on a short-term market-timing decision or ensuring that the

[77]This example highlights some of the unappreciated elements of documenting mandates. Unintended latitude may allow investment managers to "easily earn alpha" by accessing an unintentionally broad opportunity set, reporting good performance, and potentially, earning performance fees. Nevertheless, the manager is almost always acting within his or her mandate. We see the importance of properly documenting the mandate *ex ante*.

process underlying the decision is robust, aligned, risk controlled, and contributing to achievement of the objective?

We acknowledge that listening to manager presentations and messing about with market timing have more sizzle. Superintending the process and ensuring that the process is correct, however, are more closely aligned with how the beneficiary might expect the investment committee to spend its scarce GT. Being an effective fiduciary is less about the ability to technically evaluate manager selection or market-timing calls and more about managing risk and overseeing a defensible, repeatable, and documented investment process.

In their own words ...

"Good investment governance is not only the right thing to do, it makes good business sense. It requires a prudent process that ultimately puts the best interest of the customer first. We continually see assessed firms transition from poor to excellent investment governance and not only significantly reduce their fiduciary liability, but save significant amounts of money."

—*J. Richard Lynch, Director, fi360, Inc., and CEFEX*

Finally, we have discussed the role of time in the context of *governance* in this section. For completeness, the concept of time must also be considered by the fiduciary in terms of the *investment horizon*.[78] The setting of the time horizon over which to achieve the objective is central to understanding how intertemporal choices are made (Mosakowski and Earley 2000).[79] In the case of the three specific fiduciary investor contexts we are considering (DC plans, DB plans, and E&Fs), the challenges of intertemporal decision making and "myopic loss aversion" are real.[80] For DC plans, the challenge may involve cohorts of plan members journeying through various life stages, commencing with the accumulation phase through the transition years into retirement (see Basu and Drew 2009). For E&Fs, the challenge may involve grant

---

[78]For further discussion of long-term investing and potential agency issues, see Ambachtsheer (2014). For responsible entities and hedge funds, see, respectively, Bianchi (2010) and Bianchi and Drew (2010).

[79]Intertemporal choice is a characteristic of decisions in which costs and benefits are spread out over time (Loewenstein and Thaler 1989).

[80]For a full discussion of behavioral finance and myopic loss aversion over short horizons, see Benartzi and Thaler (1995).

programs, scholarships, and capital works that have different time horizons. In DB plans, the challenge is matching of liability profiles. The investment time horizon (and related commitments) are best known by the fiduciary and, therefore, must be incorporated into Step E&R and Step I of the *OPERIS* framework.[81]

Focusing on High-Value-Added Activities

Which high-value-added activities should fiduciary investors focus on? The much-cited paper by Brinson, Hood, and Beebower (1986) provided some early clues, which have been confirmed by numerous researchers, including the recent work of Scott et al. (2017). The authors reported that around 80% of the portfolio variability for international investors (in Australia, Canada, Japan, Hong Kong, the United Kingdom, and the United States) is attributable to *asset allocation policy*. **Exhibit 20** compares their results with those of Brinson et al. (1986).

These median results suggest that for outcome-oriented investors, *strategic* asset allocation decisions (as distinct from market-timing decisions) should be prioritized over less influential tasks.

Is the fiduciary of the ABC Fund spending 8 out of every 10 minutes on the long-term asset mix? Is the fiduciary solving the important asset allocation problem in a manner that maximizes the probability of achieving the objectives contained within the HIO? The agenda suggests otherwise.

Exhibit 20. Role of Asset Allocation Policy in Return Variation of Balanced Funds

Country	United States	Canada	United Kingdom	Australia	Japan	Brinson et al. (1986)
Number of balanced funds in each market sample	709	303	743	580	406	91
Median percentage of variation in actual returns explained by policy return	92%	86%	81%	89%	88%	94%

Sources: Brinson et al. (1986); Scott et al. (2017).

[81]A challenge is the seeming disconnect between the long-term investment horizons of, say, plan members and the myopic investment policies or mandates issued by plan sponsors to mutual funds and the broader investment management community (Drew 2009). Blake (1995) criticized pension funds for having an obsession with generating short-term investment returns whatever the longer-term costs.

A cursory review of the investment committee agendas for many investors suggests that the proportion of GT devoted to the asset allocation task (and testing of the investment thesis in terms of the likelihood of achieving investment objectives) is only *2 out of every 10 minutes*. We are reminded of the wisdom of economist Vilfredo Pareto, who might counsel investment committees to focus on asset allocation because most of the outcome is determined by a small number of causes.

Another aspect that should receive relatively more GT is long-term investing, which we view as a potential source of comparative advantage for the fiduciary over other investors. We use the word "potential" consciously. We have observed investment committees that, over time, suffer from a form of "cognitive dissonance" in the matter of long-term investing. This cognitive dissonance takes the form of an apparent inconsistency between the challenge the committee faces (in most cases, long-term results) and the behavior it sometimes displays (a fascination with short-term performance). As we discussed in Chapter 2, governing bodies need to have an honest conversation about what their investment beliefs are and act accordingly.

This discussion underscores the importance of fiduciary investors understanding the interactions between investment horizon, on the one hand, and alignment and delegations, on the other. This idea is neatly summarized by Neal and Warren (2015):

> Investment organizations intending to pursue long-term investing should aim to create an environment where all principals and agents along the chain of delegations are aligned, engaged on an ongoing basis, incentivized to work towards long-term outcomes, and committed to investing for the long run.

In DC plans, DB plans, and E&Fs, the level and sophistication of delegations can, for good reasons, vary wildly. Therefore, the development of a tailored, agreed-on, and understood "delegation matrix" is critical.[82] A delegation matrix shows who does what and where their authority comes from. The delegation matrix can provide clarity as to exactly where *above-the-line* strategy stops and *below-the-line* implementation begins.[83] It can be

---

[82]Neal and Warren (2015) explored various delegation models specifically for remote monitoring and immersed monitoring. According to the authors, remote monitoring, which is the more traditional approach, is undertaken through a set of contracts and protocols. Immersed monitoring involves a series of overlapping links that make use of judgment (supported by data) when the time comes to evaluate managers and are abetted by a deep understanding of investment decisions.

[83]For an excellent discussion of these issues, see Rice, DiMeo, and Porter (2012).

a catalyst for a range of important governance issues to be considered and formalized by the fiduciary. Formal delegations should be included with the investment committee papers as standard to ensure consistent application of the agreed-on process. The investment committee should remain ever vigilant as to the emergence of blind spots in the matrix.

Delegation—or the sharing of responsibility—by fiduciary investors is a critical skill.[84] This issue is of sufficient importance that we encourage governing bodies to hold an *in camera* session to reflect critically on how they delegate responsibility and whether their approach exhibits any "self-enhancement bias," which is described by Pfeffer, Cialdini, Hanna, and Knopoff 1998) as follows:

> One of the most widely documented effects in social psychology is the preference of most people to see themselves in a self-enhancing fashion. As a consequence, they regard themselves as more intelligent, skilled, ethical, honest, persistent, original, friendly, reliable, attractive, and fair-minded than their peers or the average person; they even consider themselves better and safer drivers than average after having been involved in a serious automobile accident. (p. 314)

This discussion session would, without question, be a difficult conversation. Delegating, giving up being the go-to expert, takes tremendous confidence and perspective, even in the healthiest of environments (Gallo 2012). In our experience, a source of ongoing challenge regarding delegations is ensuring consistency between *stated* investment policy and *actual* investment implementation to capture returns—an issue we explore in the next section.

Capturing Returns: Consistency between Policy and the Portfolio

The fiduciary plays the critical role in governing and *fortifying* the investment process. This role requires something more than simple compliance with regulations. It involves how the fiduciary investor operationalizes and aligns the investment organization to achieve outcomes in the presence of opacity and complexity. Neal and Warren (2015) noted:

> For multi-layered investment organizations, the challenge is to align principals and agents all along the entire chain of delegations in terms of shared mission, investment objectives, risk definitions and appetite, beliefs and cultures, and so on.

---

[84]For an interesting discussion of why delegation may not be happening, see Gallo (2012).

Neal and Warren (2015) specifically mentioned *beliefs* and cultures in the context of organizational alignment. We believe investment beliefs are an *apex* issue for the fiduciary (Chapter 2). Beliefs are important in the *OPERIS* framework because they guide the approach that the fiduciary investor takes to capture investment returns.

While there is some *positive* evidence to guide the formulation of investment beliefs, the specific challenge—finding the *best* way to capture returns—is largely a *normative* one.[85] Good governance requires the fiduciary to deliver excellence of execution (below-the-line activity) in a manner consistent with available resources and implementation capabilities, investment beliefs, and objectives.

We make two cautionary points. First, on many occasions, responses to the issue of how best to capture investment returns are framed as a *binary choice*—that is, this versus that, one or zero, all or none. One reason why this framing occurs may be the powerful incentives resulting from the "economics of the business" (Ellis 2011). Another reason may be that investment products are usually sold, not bought. Selling predisposes the conversation to a one-or-the-other-type paradigm. We encourage all governing bodies to challenge such framing and enshrine their views formally as part of their investment beliefs. We caution fiduciary investors to be wary of ideological-based framing in investment policy debates. Rarely, in our experience, do discussions that take the form of this-versus-that result in great outcomes for beneficiaries. As will be considered throughout this chapter, an objective-led, evidence-based framing of debates is consistent with a fiduciary standard of care and is best for beneficiaries.

Second, governing bodies without documented beliefs leave themselves open to the unwitting adoption of the strongest set of views among their service providers. This persuasion could result in a relatively frequent change in, say, unconscious (perhaps, low-conviction) beliefs, as investment managers are all-too-frequently hired and fired.

Some of the topics we discuss in this section have been topics of voluminous research and have led to the Nobel Memorial Prize in Economic Sciences being awarded to leading scholars in the field. In the context of Step E&R of the *OPERIS* framework, we consider only a handful of the practical

---

[85]Waring and Siegel (2005) noted the (all too common) confusion regarding many investment issues, such as alpha with beta, skill with luck, expected return with realized return, and style bets with true active bets.

Exhibit 21. Choices Relating to Execute and Resource

Choice	Category	Associated Belief
Passive vs. active	Execute	Skill premium?
Smart beta vs. not-so-smart beta	Execute	Factor premiums?
Public vs. private markets	Execute	Illiquidity premium?
Developed vs. emerging markets (EM)	Execute	EM risk premium?
Unlisted funds vs. exchange traded funds (ETFs)	Resource	Implementation efficiency
Cost vs. quality	Resource	Value for money
Physical vs. synthetic	Resource	Capital efficiency

choices that fiduciaries grapple with. In **Exhibit 21**, these choices are categorized by how they relate to Step E&R.[86]

Our objective is neither to prosecute (again) some of the most hotly contested ideas in financial economics nor to convince the reader of our views. Rather, we provide the list to assist fiduciaries in grappling with the issues related to the "best way to capture returns." We will discuss each of these points in Exhibit 21.

In their own words …

"There are real tensions between a fiduciary focus and a plan entity's business imperatives. Acknowledging those tensions—while retaining a commitment to a fiduciary focus—is an important first step. Adhering to proven governance best practices can help to ameliorate those tensions and lead to better decision making."

—*Lew Minsky, President and CEO, DCIIA*

As we work through the following issues related to the "best way" to capture returns, paths other than the ones we discuss may become apparent to the reader. In our minds, the key questions are as follows: (1) Does the fiduciary have a comparative advantage over other investors that would support

---

[86]On occasion, the line between execution and resourcing is blurred. For example, a governing body may find that using an exchange traded fund (ETF) to capture a particular return is the most efficient way. An unlisted fund may be the only way, however, in which a particular asset class can be accessed. In this instance, the choice of unlisted fund versus ETF becomes a matter of execution rather than resourcing.

one approach to capturing returns over another?[87] And (2) does the fiduciary have a belief that provides a rationale for certain behavior?[88]

Passive vs. Active. The market efficiency debate generates far more heat than light. As noted by Lo (2008), an engineer would look quizzically if asked to determine whether an engine was perfectly efficient. So we must have sympathy for the more pragmatic *degrees of efficiency*, or continuum of efficiency, approach to the issue. Malkiel's (2012) insight is important: "The efficient market hypothesis . . . does not imply that prices are always correct, or that all market participants are rational." Framing market efficiency in an either/or manner may lead the governing body to think that only two paths are worthy of consideration—capturing returns through traditional market capitalization–weighted benchmarks or capturing a skill premium through active investing.

It is not uncommon for governing bodies to be *both/and* in their approach by holding different beliefs within and among asset classes. For instance, the fiduciary may believe in holding *passive* and smart-beta exposures for public equities in developed markets but be *active* in emerging markets. Similarly, the investment policy may be passive for public markets (e.g., listed equity) and active for private markets (e.g., private equity). Such approaches to implementation are not inconsistent unless they are in conflict with the investment beliefs of the fiduciary above the line.

Smart Beta vs. Not-So-Smart Beta. The last decade or so has seen a rapid expansion in the amount of capital allocated to so-called smart-beta (or factor-based) approaches to capturing returns. It sometimes seems like there are as many different factors as there are days in the year. An important study by Harvey, Liu, and Zhu (2016) analyzed hundreds of scholarly articles on the topic of factor investing, and the authors cataloged some 316 different factors. Not one for every day of the year, but close![89] The proliferation of factors has been described by Cochrane (2011) as a "zoo of new factors."

---

[87]We acknowledge Adrian Orr, former chief executive officer of the New Zealand Super Fund, for challenging sovereign wealth funds to understand, document, and operationalize their advantages (or "endowments"). For the New Zealand Super Fund, these advantages are long horizon, certainty of liquidity, operational independence, and sovereign status. For more details, see www.nzsuperfund.co.nz/how-we-invest/endowments.

[88]This is where documenting beliefs as outlined in Chapter 2 has its benefits. If you can say why you have a belief, then you have a defensible reason to hold true to that belief. An observation we would make is that on more than one occasion in this industry, the "economics of the business" (Ellis 2011) has defined certain investment beliefs.

[89]Harvey et al. (2016) noted, "Our collection of 316 factors likely underrepresents the factor population."

From the pioneering work of Lefevre (1923) on time series and cross-sectional momentum to the value-investing paradigm of Graham and Dodd (1934), investors have long sought to understand the factors that persist in driving investment returns.[90] Similarly, some of the most common factor-based strategies—value, momentum, size, quality, volatility, and yield—are designed to capture the systematic elements of specific investment styles or strategies (as distinct from cap-weighted indexes that aim to represent the broad market beta; MSCI 2015).

Regarding the specific issue of how best to capture returns, fiduciary investors might have a positive belief regarding the benefits that accrue to systematically harvesting factors (i.e., factor premiums). In that case, some agreed-on rationale must exist for each factor selected (with supporting academic evidence as suggested in Chapter 2).[91]

The challenge for the fiduciary is to look through the asset classes to ascertain the drivers of returns. We encourage a line of inquiry that seeks to understand, *ex ante*, the types of factor premiums (or rewarded risks) that are to be harvested:

- Do, say, artificially erected barriers, regulations, or restrictions create some structural impediments to markets operating efficiently?

- Do investor biases or behavioral issues create persistent opportunities?

Answers to these questions might lead to a subsequent question about resourcing. For example, can we capture returns via an exchange traded fund (ETF), or are unlisted funds the only method of implementation? (We provide a fuller discussion of these issues later.)

These questions can perhaps be reduced to the fiduciary investor's belief (or otherwise) that the (*ex post*) drivers of past performance will persist into the (*ex ante*) future. Hsu and Kalesnik (2014) reminded us that "one cannot make intelligent choices regarding smart betas without first forming a view on which factors are for real." One way to be explicit about this issue is to have a cited investment belief in this regard (see Chapter 2).

Today, the fiduciary must have cogent answers to these questions not only for equities but also for bonds (with the rise of quality and value factors in the fixed-interest asset class) and commodities (Bianchi, Drew, and Fan 2015,

---

[90]Lefevre (1923) famously observed, "I noticed that in advances as well as declines, stock prices were apt to show certain habits, so to speak. I looked for stock prices to run on form. I had 'clocked' them. You know what I mean."

[91]Bender, Briand, Melas, and Subramanian (2013) explained that "a factor can be thought of as any characteristic relating to a group of securities that is important in explaining their return and risk."

2016).[92] Moreover, academic evidence suggests that the selection of risk factors, portfolio selection method, and investment horizon may also have material effects on resultant outcomes when investing by way of a smart-beta or factor-based approach (Bianchi, Drew, and Pappas 2017).

Although the nomenclature used for smart betas has reassuring terms—such as "harvesting," "systematic capture," and "rewarded factors"—the challenge of capturing these premiums in a transparent and repeatable manner is much harder than these terms imply. As Brakke (2016) bracingly observed,

> In terms of investor behavior, the evidence is that factor investing looks much like traditional active investing, with investors moving from factor strategy to factor strategy, depending on the environment and, of course, performance. (p. 1)

Again, this is more anecdotal evidence of cognitive dissonance on the part of investment committees—dedicated to long-term investing, until, well, they're not.

Fiduciaries can either grapple with this sort of complex issue and attempt to both navigate the competing arguments and tame the factor zoo, *or* they can delegate the matter of how best to capture returns to the parties best able to judge the merits of the strategies and then hold those parties to account. No two fiduciary bodies will make the same decision because it will be a function of the governance budget, the nature of the investment problem, and other factors. What does not change is that the governing body bears the ultimate accountability for the decision.

Public vs. Private Markets. Over the past decade, fiduciary investors have developed a growing interest in (and allocation to) private-market opportunities (such as private equity, infrastructure, and real estate). Also, to improve geometric returns, new research is looking at combining sleeves of public- and private-market exposure (such as real estate via REITs and direct holdings) in a multiasset setting (Drew, Walk, and West 2015a).

We believe that discussion of public markets versus private markets is best framed when the governing body clearly defines what are (and are not) asset classes.[93] As discussed in Chapter 4, the eligible asset classes become the

---

[92]In the case of smart-beta strategies for equities, the objective of the investment program needs to be clearly stated. Because equities typically represent the largest portion of risk allocation in multiasset portfolios, the timeframe for evaluation needs to be clear (see Chapter 7). Smart-beta approaches can be very different from traditional (market cap–weighted) methods of capturing returns. Without robust strategy, implementation, and monitoring, these approaches can deliver investment outcomes that, with hindsight, may be, well, not so smart.
[93]See the influential work of Merton (1973).

opportunity set that is modeled in our investment process (see the "Inputs" in Exhibit 10). Despite the extensive use of the term "asset class" in the vernacular of modern finance, there is a paucity of literature that genuinely attempts to define and classify its meaning.[94] The definition by Greer (1997) suggests that "an asset class is a set of assets that bear some fundamental economic similarities to each other and that have characteristics that make them distinct from other assets that are not part of that class." Several articles testing these ideas (by using various methodologies) have been presented for a range of asset classes, as follows:

- commodities: Ankrim and Hensel (1993) examined commodities as an asset class. Mongars and Marchal-Dombrat (2006) also examined commodities and argued it is a distinct asset class;

- hedge funds: Oberhofer (2001) examined whether hedge funds are an asset class or a subset of other assets;

- private equity: Fraser-Sampson (2010) provided a detailed rationale for private equity as an asset class;

- private real estate: Hudson-Wilson, Gordon, Fabozzi, and Giliberto (2005) argued the benefits of adding real estate as an asset class; and

- infrastructure—perhaps the most controversial in recent times, whether it is public or private: Bianchi, Bornholt, Drew, and Howard (2014) found that the variation of US infrastructure index returns can be readily explained by a holding of broad US stocks and the US utilities industry. Finkenzeller, Dechant, and Schafers (2010) argued that listed infrastructure is a separate asset class because it does not exhibit the same return and risk properties as real estate. Newell, DeFrancesco, and Peng (2011) showed that listed infrastructure is highly correlated with stock returns. Rothballer and Kaserer (2011) reported similar results.

The current debate regarding whether the returns from infrastructure are best captured through public (listed) or private markets is emblematic of a broader debate regarding the future of real asset investing. Some analysts have suggested that listed infrastructure is a *fake* asset class because it is fully subsumed by existing asset classes or risk factors (see Bianchi, Drew, and Whittaker 2017; Blanc-Brude, Whittaker, and Wilde 2017). **Exhibit 22** examines the idea that it is fake. As to be expected, such findings have

---

[94]The discussion in this section is based on the work of Bianchi, Drew, and Whittaker (2017). We thank and acknowledge Robert J. Bianchi at Griffith University and Tim Whittaker at EDHEC for their contributions to and insights for this important debate.

Exhibit 22. The Rise of #FakeInfra

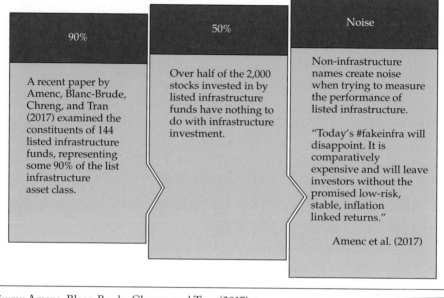

A recent paper by Amenc, Blanc-Brude, Chreng, and Tran (2017) examined the constituents of 144 listed infrastructure funds, representing some 90% of the list infrastructure asset class.

Over half of the 2,000 stocks invested in by listed infrastructure funds have nothing to do with infrastructure investment.

Non-infrastructure names create noise when trying to measure the performance of listed infrastructure.

"Today's #fakeinfra will disappoint. It is comparatively expensive and will leave investors without the promised low-risk, stable, inflation linked returns."

Amenc et al. (2017)

Source: Amenc, Blanc-Brude, Chreng, and Tran (2017).

received heavy criticism from those managing money in this asset class (see Newell 2017; Southwell 2017).

Whether an asset class is real or fake is a debate for another forum. The substantive issue is how best to capture returns—through public markets, private markets, or a combination. Fiduciaries do not have the luxury of endlessly debating what an asset class is; they must define the opportunity set so that the IPS can be resolved and the beneficiary's interests served (Chapter 5).

Investment professionals are trained to think in the twin domains of reward and risk. Consideration of how best to capture returns demands that the fiduciaries also formalize their views on risk—not simply at the asset-class level but for the total portfolio. This is best captured as an investment objective in the HIO as it will then become a criterion by which competing asset allocations are judged.

Let us agree that in a multiasset portfolio setting, equity risk is the *primus inter pares* (first among equals). So, should not the addition of, say, real assets to the portfolio be considered in terms of their contribution (or not) to diversifying equity risk, ability to access the illiquidity premium, and thus ability to improve the likelihood of achieving outcomes? If, for example, the fiduciary does not believe in the presence of an illiquidity premium, their assessment of the marginal benefit of holding real assets might not be positive.

The key issue is that fiduciary investors should be spending far more GT on managing risk exposures, and marginal benefits and costs, at the *total portfolio* level (Gupta 2016). This issue is far more relevant than second-order debates about, for example, public versus private assets.

Although private assets entail additional cost and complexity, research highlights the accretive nature of the asset class at the total portfolio level (Harris, Jenkinson, and Kaplan 2014). Before we search for any incremental yield, however, we need to satisfy ourselves that it exists. This due diligence would normally be done, as suggested in Chapter 4, when the governing body defines its opportunity set of eligible asset classes. In some cases, organizations express such strong conviction in things like the illiquidity premium that they appear in the governing body's set of investment beliefs (Chapter 2). Counterbalancing such a belief are other important considerations, such as the need for liquidity to meet cash outflow requirements and fee budgets. Again, we see the tension between a purportedly good thing (the positive illiquidity risk premium) and a competing obligation (the need to finance cash outflows). The governing body must balance these competing forces.

Assuming that the governing body has formed a positive view about the illiquidity premium—and given the increasing allocations to private markets around the world—we now consider how best to capture the illiquidity premium (an incremental yield) from private markets. In our discussions with fiduciary investors, we typically find good discipline regarding the reward-to-illiquidity ratio on *entering* private-asset transactions. Good governance would require fiduciaries not only to consider this ratio on acquisition but also to monitor how the ratio might change through time. Good governance calls for a disciplined process for exiting. The global financial crisis of 2007–2008 highlighted how suddenly the degree of illiquidity in a portfolio can change.[95]

This issue is important for the governing body because, arguably, one of the (many) effects of quantitative easing by central banks in recent times has been compression of the illiquidity premium for private assets. Investors holding long-duration assets have greatly benefited over the past decade from such compression. Therefore, a fiduciary may argue that a defensible rationale exists for the active management of private assets to dynamically manage the idiosyncratic nature of these assets over time. The higher-order issue for the fiduciary relates to whether a *skill* in capturing the liquidity premium is

---

[95]We encourage governing bodies to have a way to monitor portfolio illiquidity—either through liquidity bucketing (see Kentouris 2017) or liquidity cascades.

needed by those below the line to achieve targeted hurdle rates of return.[96] And, if so what evidence does the investment organization have that it can identify such skill *ex ante*?

Again, the central issue is not liquidity versus illiquidity. The key issue for those above the line, informed by the investment objectives in the HIO (Chapter 4), is whether those below the line can use Steps E&R and I to create a cogent investment program at the total portfolio level that clearly guides how returns are best captured. In this case, "best" is to be judged in the context of beliefs (Chapter 2) and investment objectives (Chapter 3) because no universal set of beliefs, or HIO, is objectively best. "Best" depends, in part, on the beneficiary and the investment challenge the beneficiary faces. The investment policy should formalize for those below the line:

- *aims*—including documentation regarding the role of the asset-class, intra-asset-class diversification guidelines, the sensitivity of the asset class to economic activity and public equities, and its inflation-hedging qualities;

- *expected returns*—which may be benchmark related, peer related, and/or absolute, such as CPI plus 5% per year;[97] and

- *risks*—including the policy on volatility and the risk budget; for private assets in particular, the fiduciary needs to *articulate* the organization's appetite for idiosyncratic risk, liquidity, leverage, the valuation cycle, and fees.

Clear policy about private-market exposures is required for those below the line to ensure that return hurdles are set *ex ante* and reviewed over time in light of the opportunity cost of capital. Moreover, the fiduciary must provide settings for sector exposures, manager arrangements (including country limits), and mandate structures.

Finally, a useful approach is for those above the line to recall that many of the features that make private assets attractive are the result of complexity and private, asset-level information. Unlike public markets, private-market holdings can be (dramatically) affected by the decisions made by co-investors. The governing body might assess what could happen if a patient co-investor is

---

[96]One school of thought about private assets is that once you have purchased the asset, you have basically decided the value of its future cash flows. For this reason, many investors are very careful about the price they pay for private assets. A second school of thought says that, even after the asset is bought, a manager can add significant value over time through active management of the asset. An understanding of how a manager approaches this active management is a criterion that the governing body, or its delegate, should consider in evaluating the manager during manager selection.

[97]Benchmark selection for private asset classes is the world's biggest can of worms, which we will note, but not cover, here.

no longer patient about tying up capital. Fiduciaries should keep in mind that investment returns are not only a function of the economics of the underlying business.

In short, a well-functioning, collaborative, and trust-based *culture* between those above and those below the line can generate significant value. We would go so far as to assert that such a culture would be a source of comparative advantage for the fiduciary investor.

Developed vs. Emerging Markets. Equities are a key return and risk driver of portfolios governed by fiduciaries, and historically, equity portfolios have been heavily home biased. Some portfolios still are. Globalization, however, has nudged investors to think about return drivers outside of their home countries.[98] A popular way of approaching global diversification within equities (and, increasingly, in other asset classes) is by investing in emerging economies.

The phrase "emerging markets" (EM) was coined by Antoine van Agtmael in 1981.[99] Setting aside the important definitional debate regarding EM (e.g., is EM defined by region or by income; what about frontier markets?), EM appears to form a significant portion of the opportunity set for fiduciary investors both now and in the future. So, what is the best way to capture the EM risk premium across the universe of eligible securities?

Although we explore the issues related to the development of investment strategy for EM in this section, keep in mind the potential for "silo" thinking in regard to sub-asset-classes. To avoid such thinking, the governing body needs to be clear about such issues as how including EM equities in the opportunity set facilitates *capturing the equity risk premium.*

Fiduciaries do not need to become subject-matter experts in EM equities in order to invest in them. They do need to govern a process, however, in which the case can be made or refuted that the EM risk premium will assist with the achievement of investment objectives (Chapter 3) in the HIO (Chapter 4). Therefore, fiduciaries need to be aware of some of the practical governance considerations when including sub-asset-classes, such as EM equities. For example:

- *Typology*—Is categorizing equities into developed versus EM equities the right way to think about the total opportunity set for equities?

- *Heterogeneity*—Each emerging economy has its own characteristics, opportunities, and risk. *Prima facie*, implementing an allocation to, say,

---

[98]For an excellent discussion of multiasset investing in the Asia-Pacific region, see Gupta (2016).
[99]A description of Van Agtmael's work can be found in "An Emerging Challenge" (2010).

public equities in Chile or Poland is a very different proposition from doing so in, say, India. Does the organization have the capabilities to assess and manage such variations *within* a sub-asset-class?

- *Access*—Should we capture returns via a broad EM index or allocate capital to a country-specific active (or passive) manager, or both? Indexing provides broad diversification, and allocations to specific areas or countries may provide the opportunity to hire or acquire skills to take advantage of the particular country's idiosyncrasies. In short, each method of capturing EM returns brings with it its own risks. It is the role of the fiduciary to interrogate the investment case.

- *Portfolio construction*—Is the allocation to EM a source of diversifying market return (a beta) or an opportunity set within which to earn a skill premium? Put another way, is EM a beta play or an alpha play or some combination of the two?

- *Implementation approach*—Depending on the answers to the previous questions, the fiduciary might be drawn to a particular implementation approach (see Chapter 7). For example, an index exposure to EM without any physical presence in the country is relatively easy to achieve by using a delegate of the governing body. Active management, in contrast, is challenging without a physical presence in the country.[100]

Finally, a variety of below-the-line issues regarding EM investing have not been explored here, including hard versus local currency,[101] to hedge or not to hedge, and the rapid growth in the issuance of sovereign and corporate bonds and loans. Many of these nuances will be decided by the governing body with advice or will be delegated to internal or external management.

Unlisted Funds vs. Exchange Traded Funds. Concerning this decision, the reader might fairly ask, what's the fuss? Why are we even debating this? Passive beta for, say, US equities can be easily accessed via mutual funds or ETFs. Providers such as the Vanguard Group offer both structures and the same methodologies to capture returns.[102] Surely, this decision is a no-brainer, a simple operational matter best delegated to management.

---

[100]Fiduciary investors should also control the EM indexes against which performance is benchmarked. At times, the concentration in market cap–weighted benchmarks in EM can be particularly backward looking (and with heavy exposure to commodities and manufacturing).
[101]See Wojcik, MacDonald-Korth, and Zhao (2017) for the financial geography of foreign exchange trading.
[102]We thank and acknowledge Kathryn Young, CFA, for her insights regarding this issue.

Even when the underlying exposures of two instruments are the same (or substantially the same), certain issues require policy guidance for those charged with below-the-line implementation. These policy issues include the fiduciary investor's views on

- investment horizon,

- ongoing investment management fees,

- transaction costs, and

- the tax implications of capturing returns in the various structures.

Analysis of the combined effect of these four factors is far from straightforward. Consider, for example, the impact of the redemption process on the taxation of returns. In the case of an investor using unlisted funds, the redemption from other investors in the pool can trigger a capital gains tax (CGT) liability for all investors. In the ETF context, one investor's decision to redeem (sell) has little impact on other investors holding the same ETF. These ETF units are not canceled but rather are purchased by other investors at the prevailing market price.

ETFs may be favorable for fiduciary investors who prefer their CGT liability to be deferred into the future—with more money deployed in markets for as long as required (i.e., a form of capital efficiency). Both instruments pay the same tax rate on the gains, but the timing of the liability can be different. So, the present value of the tax paid over time is different. Ultimately, developing above-the-line guidance to address these matters can be largely resolved through clarity of (to name but a few)

- legal personality of the investor,

- taxation status of the investor,

- the fee budget, and

- the cash flow profile.

Fiduciary investors know all too well that beneficiaries receive after-fee, after-tax returns. A combination of good investment strategy and sensible management should translate into improved outcomes for the investment objectives (HIO; Chapter 4). We encourage fiduciaries to consider issues of implementation efficiency when formulating their views on the best way to capture returns. The effective fiduciary balances execution (capturing returns) with the resourcing required to efficiently execute the plan. As with the investment objectives outlined in the HIO, this balancing act involves trade-offs.

Cost vs. Quality. A classic trade-off facing the fiduciary is cost versus quality. One issue is whether a positive relationship might exist between cost and quality. Can we build a simple economic model in which higher costs incurred by the customer yield higher quality? If the management expense ratio is used as a proxy for cost, risk-adjusted returns as a proxy for quality, and the beneficiary as a proxy for the customer, evidence from the investment management industry would reject the hypothesis in a simple model (Malkiel 1995; Gruber 1996; Drew and Stanford 2003; Harbron, Roberts, and Rowley 2017). A less generous critique of a simple model would be that, given the evidence, the sign of the predictor should be changed from positive to negative.[103]

In this section, we consider cost and quality in the context of the best way to capture returns.[104] Specifically, we use a *continuum* approach to allow the fiduciary to control for cost and quality of activities below the fiduciary line. We view the setting of a fee budget as a critical task for the governing body in determining the resourcing required to Implement (Step I) the IPS (Chapter 5). The concept of *value for money* is important for the governing body both to fulfill its fiduciary duty and to signal to the beneficiary the value proposition of the investment organization they have a relationship with.

The very discipline of formally setting a fee budget allows the fiduciary investor to seek the benefits of scale and allows for a form of self-imposed scarcity as a discipline for the investment program. For instance, a governing body with a fee budget of, say, 20 basis points announcing that it is seeking to earn illiquidity premiums through a significant private-assets program would be inconsistent. Remember, alignment between settings within the *OPERIS* framework results in coherence between the ambitions of the governing body and their realization.

As a way to illustrate the trade-off between cost and quality, we return briefly to our earlier discussion on how best to capture the equity risk premium:

- *Traditional market cap–weighted beta*—If the objective is to capture the returns of a traditional market cap–weighted index, passive strategies are the obvious choice. Costs are very low, and quality can be gauged by simple metrics, such as tracking error. The vehicle through which access is obtained remains a matter of choice (see the previous section).

---

[103]For evidence on DC plans with respect to fees and risk-adjusted performance, see Drew and Stanford (2003).

[104]We consider the broader issues of monitoring, reporting, and review in the next two chapters.

- *Factor premiums*—If the fiduciary investor is seeking to harvest factor premiums (or smart betas) in equities, cost is a little higher than with an index strategy. Quality in this context would be the efficiency and effectiveness with which the factor is harvested. Success would have to be considered against an appropriate factor-based benchmark (*not* a traditional market cap–weighted index). The wisdom of a strategy of harvesting factor premiums can (and should) be tested, however, by comparing the results with those of a passive, cap-weighted benchmark.

- *Skill premium*—Finally, voluminous research is available on the challenges facing the fiduciary wishing to earn a skill premium through active management in equities. Such an approach requires a profound understanding of how the active manager attempts to add value over time (Schaus and Gao 2017). This decision would take more than the 30 minutes allocated in our hypothetical investment committee agenda. An issue worthy of considerable investigation is whether the investment thesis of the active manager is capacity constrained. We encourage those seeking to capture a skill premium to consider the kinds of partnerships they wish to form with active managers. If a long investment horizon is a source of comparative advantage for the fiduciary investor, it would seem to follow deep, long-horizon partnerships with a select group of active investment managers—perhaps through an equity stake or a management expense ratio that reflects the fiduciary as a cornerstone investor in the fund. This strategy encourages alignment of behavior, incentives, and outcomes.

We could apply the same ideas regarding cost, quality, and the capturing of skill premiums to private assets (such as private equity addressed earlier). Given that many fiduciary investors attempt to capture the equity risk premium—through a traditional market cap–weighted beta, factor premiums, and/or a skill premium—we encourage investment committees to provide guidance on cost and quality not only at the asset-class level but also specifically at the sub-asset-class level. Such a decision is, by design, constrained within a given fee budget set by the fiduciary to demonstrate value for money. This approach also encourages the fiduciary's scarce capital resources to be allocated below the line to capture those premiums with the highest probability of contributing to the achievement of the investment objectives (Chapter 4).

Physical vs. Synthetic. Although fiduciary investors typically do a good job of setting practical parameters through a risk budget and a fee budget, a final area worth considering for the best way to capture returns is the capital efficiency of the investment program—that is, a formal capital budget. Does the IPS provide clear guidance on whether holding the agreed investment exposures should be undertaken physically, synthetically, or both (which affects the amount of capital deployed)? Fiduciary investors want their investment capital to be working for them as efficiently as possible to provide the best probability of achieving outcomes with minimum risk.

In practical terms, does the IPS allow those below the line to consider the most efficient way to gain liquid exposures—such as equity beta—through an equity index futures contract instead of, say, an unlisted fund or ETF? Such an implementation policy would potentially free up scarce capital (and possibly a portion of the fee budget) for, say, illiquid exposures (such as an allocation to private core real estate). This approach necessitates greater-than-usual governance oversight (and resourcing) of those activities below the line that would, in effect, coordinate, deploy, and manage capital across the investment program. A fiduciary with an internal treasury-like function and a mandate to capture returns in the best way possible (where "best" is a function of capital efficiency) could provide another source of comparative advantage over other investors.

In the DB plan context, completion portfolios are commonly used to reduce the risk of mismatches between existing assets and liabilities.[105] This approach has applications in other contexts; overlays might be used to efficiently implement, say, dynamic asset allocation decisions.[106] We are aware of DC plans with very strong cash inflows. Without the ability to capture returns via synthetic means, it is virtually impossible to be fully invested at all times. Therefore, derivatives are a vital tool to capture returns and ensure capital efficiency for the benefit of a DC plan member.

Some large fiduciary investors start the process of portfolio construction in the context of a *reference portfolio*—a simple investable benchmark portfolio that guides the risk budget (and other parameters) for the actual portfolio.[107] In this context, capital efficiency, using both physical and synthetic levers, is

---

[105]For more on the role of equities and portfolio completion, we refer readers to an interesting interview with Björn Kvarnskog from Australia's Future Fund (White 2017). For more on liability-driven investing and the role of the completion manager, see Max Guimond, "Completion Management: The Capstone of an LDI Strategy," LDI Programme Series (December 2015): www.standish.com/us/en/Research-and-Insights/asset_upload_file629 _190487.pdf.

[106]For further discussion of the efficient implementation of dynamic asset allocation decisions, see Elder (2016).

[107]Reference portfolios typically take the form of an investable, liquid, public-market proxy (including some combination of growth and fixed-income betas). For a practical example, see New Zealand Super Fund's transparency regarding their reference portfolio composition at www.nzsuperfund.co.nz/how-we-invest/reference-portfolio.

central to the value proposition of the approach. We have consciously raised the issue of the capital budget last because for fiduciary investors, a capital budget requires a governance budget and sophistication (typically the purview of large sovereign wealth funds and large fiduciary investors). These ideas are rapidly gaining adoption, however, by large DC plans, DB plans, and E&Fs. Regardless of the size and scale of the fund, good investment governance demands that those above the line acknowledge the role of capital efficiency when considering the best way to capture returns.

And, as the fiduciary investor knows, capturing returns is not cost free. Unfortunately, the global fee debate is commonly framed in terms of the "money" component of a value-for-money assessments. We suggest the perhaps unpopular view that the fees paid are more than simply active investment manager remuneration; rather, they are the cost associated with pursuing an outcome.[108]

By appropriately executing and resourcing the process in Step E&R, the governing body can improve alignment with those below the fiduciary line, sharpen decision rights across the investment organization, and reduce opacity. Such a process—characterized as defensible, repeatable, and documented—provides the foundation from which implementation excellence can be pursued, which is the topic of the next chapter, Step I (**I**mplement).

Points for Reflection: Chapter 6. Below the Fiduciary Line: "The Doing"

As a fiduciary:

- Can I say that the governing body appropriately delegates responsibilities (when relevant) while retaining ultimate accountability?

- In situations in which we share responsibility with delegates, am I clear as to their decision rights?

- Can I point to evidence of a culture of beneficiary-centric decision making across the investment organization?

- Can I point to a documented chain of trusted relationships across the investment organization that is well governed?

- Am I involved in approving an investment governance budget annually?

---

[108]For a study regarding the use of tail risk hedging, see Basu and Drew (2015).

- Can I convincingly argue that our investment governance budget reflects the scale, complexity, and nature of the investment issue before the beneficiary?

- Can I show that our investment committee's use of time and resources mirrors our priorities?

- Do I ensure that asset allocation matters receive due attention? If not, why not?

- Is manager selection a source of comparative advantage for the investment committee or me? Does the presence (or absence) of this advantage determine the time spent on this activity?

- Can I recall the last time that we considered how best to execute and resource the investment program?

- Can I explain how cost considerations are incorporated into deliberations about capturing returns?

- Can I show how the governing body considers value for money in relation to investing?

7. The Many Paths to Implementation

"In general, an implementation must be *conservative* in its sending behavior and *liberal* in its receiving behavior."

—*Jon Bruce Postel*[109]

We are now entering the penultimate step in the *OPERIS* framework—Step I, Implement (see **Exhibit 23**). As discussed in previous chapters, the governing body can craft the investment strategy in a variety of ways to solve the investment challenge. The seeds of the implementation step were sown in Step E&R—executing and resourcing the investment strategy (Chapter 6). As with the crafting of investment strategy above the fiduciary line, many paths lead to implementation—a continuum stretching from outsourced through insourced.

Exhibit 23.   *OPERIS* Framework: Implement

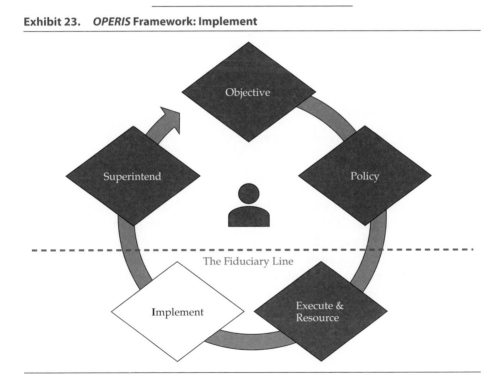

[109]Jon Bruce Postel (1943–1998) was a computer scientist known for his contributions to the development of internet standards. Quote from "Internet Protocol: DARPA Internet Program Protocol Specification," RFC 791 (September 1981): https://tools.ietf.org/html/rfc791.

Step I is the least transparent of all the steps in the investment process. It is at this point in the process that the governing body's reliance on delegations is at its greatest. During implementation, the guardian of "other people's money" literally hands that money to someone else—typically, an investment manager.[110] In Step I (Implement), links are added to the governing body's metaphorical chain of trusted relationships, a concept first introduced in Chapter 1. Not unexpectedly, any misalignment of the links in this metaphorical chain can severely damage not only Step I but also the entire investment process.

As with Step E&R, we conceptualize Step I as also being located below the fiduciary line. The colocation of these two steps below the line is important. For investment governance to go from "good to great" (to use Collins's much-quoted 2001 epithet), the governing body's efforts need to illuminate a clear path, aligned with the investment policy statement, toward implementation guided by Smith's ([1776] 1937) "anxious vigilance." In fact, achieving ongoing implementation excellence can be a source of considerable comparative advantage over other investors. In this chapter, we consider the following essential problems facing the governing body as it oversees Step I of the *OPERIS* framework:

- beauty parades, the accidental fiduciary, and insourcing;

- due diligence investigations;

- the role of the asset consultant; and

- conflicts of interest.

Before we discuss these problems, we acknowledge that they are but a subset of the complete set of implementation issues below the fiduciary line. We selected them because of their challenging and pervasive character. Selecting them is also an admission that in our professional journey, the search for the one "right" way to implement investment strategy has been futile. The effective fiduciary is pragmatic in following an implementation path, which must be led by the investment objectives and must agree with that most important concept—the hierarchy of investment objectives (HIO) in the governance of the investment process (Chapter 4).

---

[110]The reader might think the use of "guardian" in this context is gratuitous, but the fiduciaries of the sovereign wealth funds of both Australia and New Zealand—respectively, the Future Fund and the New Zealand Super Fund—are called "guardians."

Beauty Parades, the Accidental Fiduciary, and Insourcing

Traditionally, fiduciary investors have delegated some—or all—of the responsibility for the management of the beneficiary's assets to external investment managers. In this section, we explore some of the challenges of implementation paths that tend toward "outsourced" implementation and those that tend toward "insourced" implementation. We pause here to stress (again) that the fiduciary cannot outsource accountability. The governing body must have clarity (and ongoing assurance) about delegated responsibilities relating to investment implementation.

We begin with the role of beauty parades as a method of vetting investment managers to undertake implementation on behalf of the governing body. Beauty parades have played an important role in what Clark and Monk (2017) have described as the "precontract screening" of investment managers. Beauty parades provide a forum in which the investment management firm can emphasize the benefits of *its* investment process (Clark and Monk 2015). These parades allow the governing body to metaphorically "kick the tires" of a potential vendor—or as much kicking as can be done in, say, 30 minutes (see Chapter 6). Governing bodies typically work with their asset consultant to create a shortlist of managers that will "stand out from their peers, or those that will at least be a safe pair of hands" (Clare and Wagstaff 2011).[111]

We believe any manager selection process that relies heavily on a beauty pageant is largely ineffectual. As noted by Tan Bhala, Yeh, and Bhala (2016), when manager selection is based on beauty parades, the governing body may "conflate 'liking' the applicant fund manager with future good performance." The risk is that the governing body may "hard bake" representative bias into the implementation process, which prioritizes traits such as attractiveness, appearance, and personality, perhaps unwittingly, as being related to superior *future* investment performance (Tan Bhala et al. 2016). As many readers have witnessed first-hand, such a process can border on the farcical when the shortlisting criteria are based primarily on historical investment performance.[112] As Clare and Wagstaff (2011) noted, "If you have never experienced a fund management beauty parade before be prepared for lots of sharp suits and dazzling PowerPoint wizardry."

How did we get to this place? Is this really the best path to implementation?

---

[111]As we discuss later in this chapter, the criteria used to generate the shortlist are critical.

[112]An important field of academic and industry research is concerned with whether the track record of an asset manager is information rich regarding future performance—namely, the hot-hand anomaly, see Hendricks, Patel, and Zeckhauser (1993); Brown and Goetzmann (1995); Gruber (1996); Carhart (1997); and Wermers (2000).

Exhibit 24 provides a statistical look at the backgrounds of people serving in fiduciary positions. As the reader can see, the service of many of them could be described as *accidental* in nature. We do not use the term as any form of disrespect, only as descriptive of how the people became fiduciaries. As we suggested in Chapter 1, many individuals become fiduciaries as a function of their roles:

- the human resources (HR) professional who becomes a fiduciary as a result of her daily responsibilities with the company's retirement plan,

- labor representatives (or union officials) and employer representatives who are appointed to the fiduciary board of a defined-contribution (DC) plan,

- the chief financial officer who, having had a long and distinguished career as a widget counter, is an *ex officio* member of the widget company's defined-benefit (DB) plan board, or maybe

- a leading college professor of oncology who is appointed to the board of a large charitable fund that supports cancer research.

The substantive point is that, in many instances, some of those above the line have limited technical ability to independently evaluate various managers in accordance with the fiduciary obligation of care. Many fiduciaries are not in the governing body because of their technical abilities but because

Exhibit 24. **Who Are the Decision Makers? Who Are the Voting Committee Members for Administration- and Investment-Related Decisions for the DC Plan?**

Administration-Related Decisions		Investment-Related Decisions	
Job/Department	Percentage	Job/Department	Percentage
Human resources	**64.9%**	Executives (e.g., CEO, CIO, CFO)	50.3%
Executives (e.g., CEO, CIO, CFO)	50.3%	Treasury/Finance	49.7%
Treasury/finance	39.7%	**Human resources**	**42.4%**
Legal	29.8%	**Investment staff**	**37.1%**
DB plan fiduciaries	23.2%	DB plan fiduciaries	33.8%
Other	16.6%	Legal	23.8%
Investment staff	**10.6%**	Other	17.2%
Unsure	1.3%	Unsure	0.7%

Note: Multiple responses were allowed.
Source: Callan Associates (2017).

they represent a beneficiary (or group of beneficiaries). So, the term "limited" should not be taken as a criticism, merely an observation.

The information asymmetry between, say, an experienced HR professional (above the line) and a seasoned investment manager (below the line)—even with the best of professional development—is significant. To be fair to HR professionals, even for an investment professional with a PhD in financial economics and many years of experience, the most likely outcome after evaluating anything for a short time (say, 30 minutes) is debatable (see Chapter 6). In this light, manager selection by beauty pageant is a symptom of a much larger implementation problem, *not* the cause of the problem many governing bodies face.

Reliance on beauty parades (as a manager selection process) can create a cycle that compounds the impact of poor decisions over time. As observed by Arnott, Kalesnik, and Wu (2017), "Institutional investors often sell funds (or fire managers) once they have underperformed the market over the last two to three years, typically replacing them with funds or managers that recently outperformed." This sort of implementation is value destroying.[113]

We suggest that beauty parades and an overemphasis on past performance in manager selection have been a catalyst for the trend toward *insourcing* investment implementation. Up to this point, we have assumed that the fiduciary uses only outsourced investment implementation. As scale increases, however, an insourced model can reduce costs (with the fee budget being a known and significant source of cost for the governing body) and potentially mitigate some of the concerns that keep fiduciaries awake at night, including the following:

- alignment and information asymmetry;

- fee levels (base and incentive);

- risk (in all its forms) and assurance;

- environmental, social, and governance issues; and

- culture, myopia, tailoring, control, fraud, scalability, flexibility, liquidity, and many more.

---

[113]An important counterintuitive insight is provided by Arnott et al. (2017): "If a manager has performed brilliantly and the manager's assets are at record-high valuations relative to the market, investors should arguably redeem, not invest more. If a manager has performed badly and the manager's assets are at an exceptionally cheap relative valuation, investors should seriously consider topping up, rather than firing the manager. We are not suggesting that past performance is irrelevant, only that it's a terrible predictor of future prospects. Likewise, past success is not always a sell signal."

Fiduciary investors can evaluate the decision to partially (or fully) insource investment implementation by using traditional business methodologies (such as net present value [NPV] calculation). We encourage the fiduciary to consider the following issues regarding the decision to insource or not:

- Will insourcing investment management increase the probability of the investment organization achieving its investment objectives? As we could see from the HIO in Chapter 4, objectives can be about much more than simply time-weighted returns.

- Will the decision to insource be positive in an NPV sense? Again, finding an answer would require more than simply evaluating the net cash flow resulting from fee savings; it also would have to formally incorporate cash flows associated with noninvestment staff, technology, systems, processes, and heightened governance *resourcing*. Net cash flow can be estimated with (some) accuracy; the much harder question is the selection of the discount rate.

- Does the broad investment organization have the maturity and necessary infrastructure to support running internal investment management mandates? What would be the "interaction costs" of insourcing for the rest of the organization?[114]

In their own words ...

"Appropriate resources can improve efficiency . . . [allowing] focus on participant outcomes and plan utilization."

—*Chris Anast and Sue Walton,*
Senior Vice Presidents, Capital Group

The move to insourcing, as expected, also requires due diligence to be applied to vendors (benchmarking services, order management, risk management, performance, and data vendors) and a range of other operational and

---

[114]An excellent note by Williams (2017) explores insourcing (and associated costs and benefits) for large fiduciary investors, specifically DC plans in Australia.

regulatory issues. In addition, items such as culture and people are harder to capture in an NPV analysis evaluating an insourcing decision.[115]

In this regard, we think of culture and people in a broad sense. Would the move to insourcing investment implementation result in more conservatism in the investment approach (e.g., we cannot lose money)? The same variation in performance observed in outsourced investment managers will inevitably be observed in internal investment processes. Now the fiduciary faces the challenge of when to fire internal staff. How would the governing body handle this issue? Would research and investment innovation be sacrificed on the altar of cost efficiency? Would a culture of *empire building* within the investment organization flourish? How would the culture of, say, a charitable or not-for-profit organization, coexist with the culture (and remuneration) of an internal investment team?

For us, these really difficult questions deserve much consideration (and critical reflection) by the governing body, even if that body is not the party that makes the eventual decisions in the particular circumstances (because it has been delegated to someone else). Williams and Cornelius (2016) described the deliberations regarding the insourcing of investment as "the asset owners' conundrum."

The outsource-versus-insource investment implementation debate is an important one. Although any new business venture (and associated business planning) is risky, the decision to insource will be financed indirectly by those to whom the fiduciary duty is owed (i.e., the beneficiary). Therefore, due diligence on any decision should arguably be made in accordance with fiduciary obligations of care. One might even argue that the fiduciaries ought to behave like they are protecting an equity investment owned directly by the beneficiary (which it essentially is).

The move to insourcing also requires a high level of organizational maturity to ensure its success. What happens when, say, the governing body assesses the balance of benefits and costs of internal management as *inferior* to the external equivalent (see the Harvard Management Company as a living

---

[115]We believe that risk management deserves a special mention in this context. Fiduciary investors do not have the long risk management experience of banks, mainly because of differences in regulatory treatment, which in turn, resulted from fiduciary investors typically not being highly leveraged organizations like banks (Drew and Walk 2016).

case study)?[116] Our working hypothesis is that it may be far more difficult to dislodge an entrenched internal process within the investment organization than it is to issue a termination letter to an external party.

These remarks are not intended to be discouraging for fiduciary investors. Far from it. The extraordinary growth in funds under management in the investment organizations we recount in this book—DC plans, DB plans, and endowments and foundations—could enable insourced investment implementation to become another source of comparative advantage that the fiduciary holds over other investors.

Due Diligence Investigations

Due diligence investigations are a vital component of the fiduciary's overall process of assurance. These evaluations typically begin with consideration of a screen based on the manager's investment performance: performance measurement (track record), attribution (the "how"), and performance appraisal (skill or luck). From this initial screen, good practice considers wider matters, such as people, organizational capacity, investment process, and broad operational due diligence concerns. Good resources are available to fiduciaries for the standardized process of manager due diligence; they ensure that a consistent, evidentiary process is followed for both external and internal managers.[117] Brakke's (2016) work again underscores the importance of being

---

[116]At the time of writing, Chung and Lim (2017, for example) are reporting on the Harvard Management Company's 2017 annual report in the *Wall Street Journal*. This provides those above the line with a living case study of the costs of going, perhaps against the current tide, from a predominantly insourced model to an outsourced design. Chung and Lim quoted the new CEO, N. P. "Narv" Narvekar, saying that the returns from the endowment are a "symptom of deep structure problems" with the US$37 billion endowment fund. Chung and Lim (2017) note that "Mr. Narvekar said the endowment was working to be viewed as a reliable client after years of leadership churn that had cast its appeal as an investor into question. 'It will take about five years to remake its illiquid (private) investments and two years for its public markets,' he wrote. It will also take time to upsize investments with money managers who are not accepting much money anymore." We will watch this unfolding story with much interest—what an interesting topic for a (Harvard) case study!

[117]An excellent resource has been developed by the Australian Institute of Superannuation Trustees entitled "Investment Manager Operational Due Diligence Guidance Note" (AIST 2016). We also recommend the outstanding work by fi360 (2016) in developing their "Prudent Practices for Investment Stewards" and Tipple's (2010) work on the tangible "4 P's" (people, process/philosophy, portfolios, and performance) and the intangible "4 P's" (passion, perspective, purpose, and progress) is required reading for CFA® Program candidates. A good practice is to formally incorporate operational due diligence matters into Tipple's framework to evaluate such issues as compliance systems; operations, trading, and technology platforms; third-party vendors; disaster recovery; organizational structure, ownership, and incentives; and the investment managers' key service providers, including banking arrangements, custodian, and auditors (hopefully, you will find no "auditor shopping").

forward looking when undertaking the due diligence required to implement the investment strategy:

> Due diligence in manager selection has become too much of a standardized documentation process. It should be an investigative discovery process. Rather than focusing on past performance of individual managers, the focus in due diligence should be on the defining characteristics of the investment management organizations where the managers work. In the long run, organizational structure, not past performance, is likely to drive future performance. (p. 1)

The decision by the governing body to add another link to its metaphorical chain of trusted relationships (i.e., appointment of an investment manager) requires high-quality manager due diligence. This comes at a considerable cost (e.g., governance time, internal resources, asset consulting fees).[118] This is another practical example of the importance of due diligence in the governance budget of the fiduciary investor.

As economists, we view the resources dedicated to due diligence as being a sort of "production possibilities frontier" for the investment program—a way of answering the question, what's possible? Low budgets will naturally lead to an implementation path that is largely passive. In such a model, the prudent practice is to allocate much of the budget to routine operational due diligence. As Brakke (2016, p. 2) wisely reminded us, however, what seems on the surface like "fairly modest" due diligence requirements for passive investing still require "careful consideration." **Exhibit 25** showcases Brakke's thoughts on due diligence in manager selection. When more of the governance budget is made available for due diligence, additional paths to implementation emerge.[119]

Fiduciaries with strong investment beliefs (Chapter 2) will have due diligence processes and procedures that are consistent with those beliefs. For example, a governing body that has a strong belief in the illiquidity premium and the role of private assets in portfolios would be expected to devote

---

[118]For instance, if the due diligence process is being largely conducted by staff within an investment organization, good practice would require at least two senior investment staff members to conduct every evaluation. This practice assists with mitigating key-person risk, fraud, and potential misadventure. For specialist asset classes, processes and managers, asset consulting advice, and academic advice might also be sought as standard.

[119]We hold the work of Tom Brakke in very high regard. His blog on the research puzzle (see http://researchpuzzle.com/)—is the gold standard regarding the practical challenges of due diligence and investment manager selection. Brakke (2016) cautions that, when evaluating claims of true skill, "although a tremendous amount of information is available on active managers, getting useful, differentiated information is difficult, time-consuming, and expensive." Do we, as fiduciary investors, have the governance budget to implement an investment program dedicated to earning, say, the skill premium across all asset classes?

Exhibit 25.   On Manager Selection: Organizational Alpha versus Portfolio Alpha

Qualitative versus Quantitative Information

"We need to favor qualitative information over quantitative measures. Reputation is a lagging factor, and the real organization is hidden from us. We must uncover it—that is what due diligence is all about. I suggest grading organizations ex-performance."

The Perils of the Popularity Cycle

"We should buy and sell against the popularity cycle by basing decisions on the quality of the organization, not what its recent performance has been, and analysts should act as if they have 10-year investment horizons."

Adding Value for Clients

"To add value on behalf of clients, we have to change the way we are making decisions. The focus should be on the organization and how decisions are made. We should be looking for organizational alpha, not portfolio alpha."

Source: Brakke (2016).

---

a significant portion of its governance budget to due diligence because the investments that flow from that body's beliefs necessitate doing so.

In many instances, much of the heavy lifting regarding due diligence and manager selection is conducted on behalf of the fiduciary by one or more asset consultants. That such important functions are outsourced to an asset consultant emphasizes the fact that fiduciaries must be comfortable with the expertise of their delegates and must have independent processes in place to evaluate performance. We explore these ideas in the next section.

The Role of the Asset Consultant

Asset consultants can play a critical and, at times, contested role in supporting the fiduciary investor. We suggest that the most substantial part of the "contested" nature of this relationship can (as in so many areas) be attributed to the imprecision of decision rights (Chapter 6)—a theme that will permeate this and the next section. We cannot overstate the importance of asset consultants in Step I of the *OPERIS* framework. Many asset consultants are the delegated gatekeepers between the fiduciary investors and their investment managers. **Exhibit 26** provides a 2017 survey of the role of asset consultants in DC plans. When the relationship is at its best, the asset consultant can be a "medium" through which governing boards learn about developments in their field, thereby "empowering" the fiduciary (Clark and Monk 2017). Asset consultants can greatly assist the fiduciary to ensure that the metaphorical chain of trusted relationships is aligned. And, as some have attributed to Voltaire (and others, to Spiderman), "with great power comes great responsibility."

Exhibit 26.   The Role of Asset Consultants in DC Plans: A Recent Survey of 165 DC Plan Sponsors

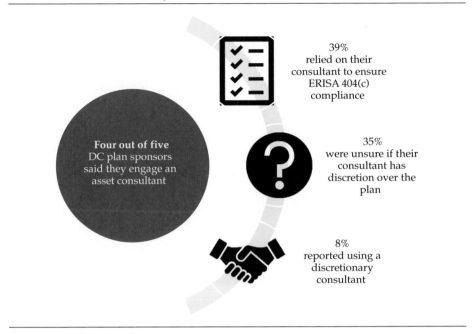

39%
relied on their
consultant to ensure
ERISA 404(c)
compliance

Four out of five
DC plan sponsors
said they engage an
asset consultant

35%
were unsure if their
consultant has
discretion over the
plan

8%
reported using a
discretionary
consultant

Source: Callan Associates (2017).
Note: The plans were primarily large and mega 401(k) plans.

The governing body can take many paths to implementation. Some fiduciary investors engage asset consultants to provide an outsourced chief investment officer (or fiduciary management) function, usually abbreviated to OCIO—completely outsourcing all investment implementation. This path is popular in the endowment and foundation arena, where a third party manages the day-to-day running of the investment portfolio. Some fiduciary investors invest through the implemented consulting service of an asset consultant; this path is functionally equivalent to an OCIO. Others retain an asset consultant to undertake asset allocation strategy and manager selection. Large fiduciary investors may have a panel of asset consultants and engage consultants only for matters on which their specific expertise is highly regarded (say, an asset consultant specializing in alternatives). Some fiduciary investors have no ongoing relationship with an asset consultant; instead, they resource their internal team (and may use an asset consultant only for periodic external review)—effectively insourcing all investment implementation.

The continuum of outsourced to insourced approaches to implementation (and all the potential paths in between) must be considered in light of the fact that implementation decisions are rarely static. Consider for a moment how investors' beliefs *and* approaches to capturing returns have evolved since Markowitz's original work.[120] Investment markets are, by their nature, dynamic. Ongoing investment implementation resourcing and dynamism are thus inextricably linked. Therefore, governing boards are also constantly evaluating, testing, and in a controlled way, experimenting with their approaches to implementation. In fact, the governing body may decide at a certain juncture that a hybrid path to implementation should be followed for a particular asset class.[121]

As we know, change of any kind—in this case, the implementation path—can create ambiguity of roles and responsibilities. Clark and Monk (2015) recently observed that the relationship between governing bodies and their asset consultants is worryingly "characterized by ambiguity." And just as the costs associated with conducting investment manager due diligence can be substantial, so too can asset consulting fees account for a substantial portion of the fiduciary investor's governance budget.[122]

Obviously, specifying with precision the decision rights of the delegated asset consultant is important if the investment strategy is to be successfully implemented, but such rights are also emerging as an area of interest for *regulators*. Regulators are increasingly examining the role and responsibilities of asset consultants and have flagged a range of issues they are concerned about. The following statement from Britain's Financial Conduct Authority (FCA 2017) discusses managing conflicts of interests:[123]

---

[120]For an interesting discussion on the impact of Markowitz (1952) on professional practice, see Kaplan and Siegel (1994) and Frankfurter and Phillips (1994), both in the same edition of *Journal of Investing*.

[121]By "hybrid path," we mean the governing body is using controlled experimentation of different implementation paths in a prudent way. For instance, we could imagine a megahypothetical DC plan that for many years has used a good external manager for, say, private infrastructure transactions slowly building an internal capability in that area. The governing body would need to keep its assurance processes in place for the external manager (outsourced) and, at the same time, crank up an equivalent level of assurance for its emerging internal (insource) capability—a form of hybrid implementation.

[122]For instance, Hoyle (2017) reported that, for 2016–2017, the California Public Employees' Retirement System (CalPERS) expects to spend more than US$20 million on asset consulting fees alone (and around US$896 million in total external manager fees). We commend the board of administration and executive officers of CalPERS for their transparency regarding this issue.

[123]We regard the recent final report by the United Kingdom's peak regulator, the Financial Conduct Authority (FCA 2017) as a must read for those above the line when formulating policy around the role of the asset consultant (more commonly referred to as "investment consulting" in the United Kingdom). See Leahy and Drake (2017) for an excellent summary of the FCA's (2017) report. See also Smith (2016) for a discussion on the current state of the asset consulting industry in Australia.

Although there are inherent conflicts of interest in the investment consulting business model, these must be properly managed to prevent distortions in competition that disadvantage investors. Our interim findings suggested that there were differences between firms in how they were managing these conflicts. We are encouraged that a number of asset consultants' responses suggested they are improving their policies to manage conflicts of interests. However, we are still concerned about how effectively conflicts are being managed, particularly conflicts that arise from offering both advice and fiduciary management.

Our motivation in raising these issues is *not* to take one side over another. We are motivated to shed light on some of the reasons why such ambiguity may arise when governing bodies consider the many paths to implementation in Step I. Large fiduciary investors are increasingly insourcing functions, reducing demand for the services of asset consultants, and thus placing downward pressure on their fees. In parallel, fiduciary investors and investment managers are attracting asset consultants to work for them as employees. These currents conspire to push consultants to generate alternative sources of income, such as fees for manager selection or implemented consulting.

The simultaneous provision of *above-the-line* strategic advice and *below-the-line* implementation activity creates the impression of a conflict of interest. This becomes especially apparent when the above-the-line strategic advice is both increasingly low margin for the consultant, yet valuable in that it can influence settings below the line (e.g., a preference for active management). The temptation that is created for the consultant without scruples is to create a demand for its own, more lucrative, below-the-line services. At firms that have delegated roles and responsibilities, a belief in active management among the governing fiduciaries ought to be sincere, not merely a function of the "economics of the business" (Ellis 2011). We say this knowing full well that the vast majority of asset consultants are excellent, ethical professionals.

We argue that, in the absence of good governance (Step O and Step P *above* the fiduciary line), the asset consultant will be forced to fill the governance vacuum to implement the investment program. This should *not* be the responsibility of the asset consultant alone. The beneficiaries are best served by the fiduciary's ensuring that they have an investment governance process—including the effective employment of asset consulting resources—to fulfill their fiduciary duty to the beneficiary. Without a defensible, repeatable, and documented investment governance process, the governing body can only *hope* that asset consultants are aligned with the beneficiary. Hope is not an investment policy. Hope does not achieve objectives. And hope is not a defense when the fiduciary is on the witness stand.

We encourage readers to seek out those fiduciary investors who provide an evidentiary basis for claiming best practice regarding the roles and responsibilities of their delegated asset consultants. For example, CalPERS exhibits excellence as a fiduciary investor on the topic of asset consulting and investment implementation.[124] The point is that excellence *and* independence of asset consulting advice costs something; it is up to the governing body to decide the extent of the governance budget they wish to dedicate to such peace of mind.

Conflicts of Interest

It perhaps goes without saying that conflicts of interest are, unfortunately, inherent in fiduciary investing. David Swensen, quoted in CFA Society of the UK (2013), neatly summarized that "the whole investment management area is cluttered with conflicts of interest and agency problems." Those with deep investment governance experience and extensive networks—that is, those with potentially the highest conflicts—may in fact be best placed to help the governing body obtain the assurance it requires regarding investment implementation.

The identification, monitoring, management, and mitigation of conflicts—both real and perceived—should be more than simply a standing item on the board agenda (such as a fiduciary declaration or responsible person declaration) for Step I of the *OPERIS* framework. We assume that a standard suite of policies—including a code of conduct, gifts policy, client confidentiality policy, and personal investing policy—are in place and are defensible. Those governing bodies striving for best practice in the management of conflicts of interest must exhibit an "anxious vigilance" (Smith [1776] 1937) that is formally signaled across the investment organization. From the chair and members of the governing body through management and all service providers, a shared commitment to managing conflicts of interest must be present.

How well does the fiduciary govern potential conflicts of interest with, say, investment managers, asset consultants, accountants, actuaries, lawyers, insurers (including instances in which insurances are provided to plan members), banks, custodians, and in the endowment and foundation context,

---

[124]In terms of examples of good practice on this issue, we formally acknowledge and commend the transparency of CalPERS, which recently released its "Review of Survey Results on Board Investment Consultants." See the relevant board submission (CalPERS 2017a) and the accompanying survey results (CalPERS 2017b).

major donors?[125] Again many excellent resources and prudential standards are available to assist in policy development for fiduciary investors (such as APRA 2013b). We acknowledge that this topic is worthy of a book-length exploration.[126] Fiduciary investors have a responsibility to ensure that their reputation is not compromised by poorly managed, real or perceived, conflicts of interest through the implementation of the investment strategy.

A Final Word

We know that investment implementation is not free, but "good" investment implementation is priceless. It seems that holding investment beliefs is one thing (Chapter 2), but successfully implementing those beliefs is quite another matter.[127] Even if we were to assume that significant governance resources were dedicated to due diligence investigations, decision rights for the asset consultant were clear, and an "anxious vigilance" (Smith [1776] 1937) was demonstrated by the investment organization to manage real and perceived conflicts of interest, alignment in the chain of trusted relationships still might not be achieved.

In Australia, we use the colloquial expression "bush lawyer" to describe someone who is completely unqualified to provide legal opinion but does so anyway. The bush lawyer might say, "You do not go to jail for bad outcomes, you do go to jail for bad process."[128] The substantive point is that good practice in investment implementation (and investment governance in general) requires a significant, ongoing commitment to process improvement. This foundational work must be undertaken above the fiduciary line in Steps O and P and must then inform activities in Steps E&R and I below the line.

So how does the governing body close the loop? What is the place of Step S (**S**uperintend) at which point we move back above the fiduciary line? In Chapters 8 and 9, we explore the concept of the fiduciary "closing the loop." We make the case that the role of governing bodies as superintendents of the investment governance process is as much about the alignment (and clarity) of roles and responsibilities across the investment organization as it is about technical matters (such as performance evaluation).

---

[125]One situation that can be "tricky" is when an asset consultant is appointed to advise on, say, asset allocation (**Step P**) and manager selection (**Step I**) but is also used to monitor the fiduciary investor's performance, sorry, *their* performance (**Step S**).

[126]See Paul and Kurtz (2013) as these issues relate to nonprofit boards.

[127]As neatly observed by Brakke (2016), "In most organizations, I do not see the necessary resources, or the proper organization of resources, to act on that belief."

[128]In no way do these "bush lawyer" remarks constitute legal advice.

Points for Reflection: Chapter 7. The Many Paths to Implementation

As a fiduciary:

- Given the many paths to implementing an investment strategy (from outsourced through to insourced), can I point to a rationale for why our approach is the best way to deliver the HIO?

- Can I explain simply the steps that have been taken to align investment implementation with our investment policy statement?

- Do I consider the risk of representative bias when involved in manager selection?

- Will insourcing investment management increase the probability of the investment organization achieving its investment objectives? Can I point to a well-documented, evidentiary approach to formulating our views regarding this issue?

- Am I involved in regular assessments of the balance of benefits and costs of external management versus an internal equivalent? Can I point to the decision rules we use to make these trade-offs?

- Am I satisfied that our governance budget is sufficient to oversee an investment program that seeks to earn a skill premium across, say, all asset classes? Can I point to evidence that this question has been formally considered?

- Do I have a clear understanding of the nature of our relationship(s) with our asset consultant(s)? Can I point to a mechanism for resolving any ambiguity that may exist in such relationships?

- Can I practically illustrate how the asset consultant's role is aligned with achieving the HIO?

- Am I satisfied that we have a process to disclose and resolve (real and perceived) conflicts of interest with our investment managers, asset consultants, accountants, actuaries, lawyers, insurers (including instances in which insurances are provided to plan members), banks, custodians, and in the endowment and foundation context, major donors?

8. Closing the Loop: Superintending Roles and Responsibilities

"Everything that *can* be counted does not necessarily count; everything that counts *cannot* necessarily be counted."

—*Albert Einstein[129]*

Within the *OPERIS* framework, the fifth and final step is, as shown in **Exhibit 27**, **S**uperintend (from the Latin, to oversee).[130] The reader might think that "superintend" is an unusual choice of word when alternatives such as *supervise* are available. Our rationale is that, other than its appropriate technical meaning—"to oversee"—superintend suggests a sense of formality

Exhibit 27.   *OPERIS* Framework: Superintend, Part 1

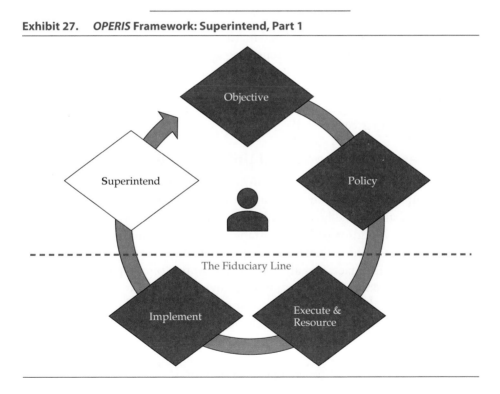

---

[129]Nathan Palmer, "Einstein Was a Qualitative Researcher," *Sociology in Focus* (3 November 2014): http://sociologyinfocus.com/2014/11/einstein-was-a-qualitative-researcher/.

[130]Cresswell (2010) explained that the Latin *intendere* means intend, extend, direct, literally to stretch towards; *superintendere* means to oversee.

and accountability.[131] In this light, the governing body is the ultimate authority with the accountability to *superintend* the governance process.

In this chapter, we make the case that superintending is something more than basic compliance and investment reporting (while acknowledging the important role that both of these activities play in assurance; see Chapter 9). To Superintend requires the governing body to target investment objectives (as specified in the hierarchy of investment objectives [HIO]; Chapter 4) *and* regularly evaluate whether the investment policy is achieving those objectives. In this chapter we specifically consider

- outcomes that are unknown and unknowable,

- the governing body as superintendent,

- compliance with mandates, and

- the journey from risk silos to risk assurance.

We do not specifically consider matters of performance evaluation and other important issues, such as reporting and review, in this chapter—we leave those matters to Chapter 9. Our motivation is to encourage governing boards to begin thinking about Step S, *Superintend*, with the big picture in mind—that is, investment objectives. As this chapter (and the next) develops, we will move into greater detail.

Outcomes Are Unknown and Unknowable

The challenge facing the fiduciary investor is that, particularly over short horizons, investment outcomes are unknown and largely unknowable. Is the fiduciary investor in the business of taking risk? Yes. Can there be a confluence of bad luck and/or bad circumstances and/or bad markets? Yes. When outcomes are uncertain, a defensible, repeatable, and documented investment process is critical; in fact, it is all that one has to rely on. Step S is about closing the loop—monitoring, reporting, and review. At this step in the process, the governing body *Superintends* the investment process, above the fiduciary line, and considers questions such as the following:

- Are we on track to achieve the investment objective?

- Do we need a midcourse change of direction?

---

[131]In the State of Queensland, Australia, where we live, "superintendent" is a senior police officer rank.

Answers to these questions typically involve some form of trade-off for the governing body.[132] For instance, the compression of real interest rates over the past decade has resulted in the present value of future liabilities being materially larger today than in the past. As we stated in Chapter 3, meeting these liabilities (commitments) requires a trade-off that will require the fiduciary investor to, for example,

- acquire a larger asset base (not an option in many circumstances),

- aim for much higher expected returns and "push the boat out" on risk, or

- have a difficult conversation with the beneficiaries—acknowledging that the probability of meeting the investment objective is negligible and that the beneficiaries will receive less than promised.[133]

Let's consider a recent real-world version of such trade-offs that has been played out in the media. In testimony, Michael S. Rawlings, the mayor of Dallas, said that the city's unfunded pension liabilities were of such a scale that the city might "walk . . . into the fan blades (of municipal bankruptcy)" (Rawlings quoted in Walsh 2016). An unpalatable trade-off must be made. If one thing can be learned from the parlous state of many US public pension plans, it is that deferring such decisions to a later date rarely results in a better outcome. As we suggested in Chapter 7, hope is not a strategy.

We raise the Dallas experience as being emblematic of what Step S is about. Achieving investment objectives is the *raison d'être* of the fiduciary investor. Good practice demands that fiduciary investors find an appropriate balance between dedicated measurement and monitoring of the outcome (say, meeting liabilities) and governing the inputs (say, manager performance).

Governing inputs is a necessary but insufficient condition to achieving investment outcomes. We can envision a situation in which the inputs may have been excellent (best in class, well governed, strongly aligned), but because of, say, underfunding and political realities, the fiduciary was induced into taking more risk than the inputs could reasonably sustain. Governing bodies must balance monitoring the details (say, individual investment manager returns) *and* the bigger picture (progress toward investment objectives as expressed in the HIO; see Chapter 4).

---

[132]If the beneficiary had a sufficient corpus (assets) to meet their needs (liabilities) today and into the future, the role of the fiduciary would be reduced to an immunization issue—that is, an income-only investment strategy (Schaus 2010). Few fiduciary investors have this luxury.

[133]Lin (2017) noted that "increasingly, pension costs consume 15% or more of big city budgets, crowding out basic services and leaving local governments more vulnerable than ever to the next economic downturn." The upshot is some unpalatable choices (and liabilities of all kinds) for "someone" (read "the fiduciary") in the not-too-distant future.

In their own words ...

"Retirement systems around the world, specifically social security-type benefit programs, are facing funding shortfalls and undergoing strain. As a result, people are becoming increasingly responsible for their long-term financial security—and that requires saving and planning."

—Catherine Collinson, President,
Transamerica Center for Retirement Studies

The Governing Body as Superintendent

When we are asked by fiduciary investors to give one—and only one—priority that must be monitored with "anxious vigilance" (Smith [1776] 1937), we point to the oversight of the roles and responsibilities across the investment process. As discussed previously, the *OPERIS* framework tells us that the investment process is only as strong as its weakest link (Chapter 6). In our experience, when any (or all) of the five steps are under stress (regardless of whether the source of the stress is endogenous, exogenous, or both), the problem can typically be linked (if only in part) to the ambiguity of roles and responsibilities.

So, how can the fiduciary investor oversee roles and responsibilities? Where is the best place to begin? We start by surveying key groups across the investment organization to form what we call an "*OPERIS* stack."

The *OPERIS* Stack. Most fiduciary investors receive incredibly detailed information that is intended to be used for monitoring, say, investment manager performance (see Chapter 9) and how that performance is tracking in aggregate against investment objectives (perhaps in the form of an HIO). But is the fiduciary monitoring how the fiduciary and the delegates are discharging their roles and responsibilities? We have developed a simple exercise to look at monitoring, in a way not usually used, by "stacking" how different groups in the investment process view their roles and responsibilities across the investment process. The stack shown in **Exhibit 28** illustrates this idea. First, we gather all those serving:

- *above the line*—we run separate exercises for the governing body (and their investment committee, where it exists);

- *below the line (internal)*—we arrange additional separate exercises for internal investment staff (say, the chief investment officer and investment strategy team) and internal investment managers; and

Exhibit 28.   The *OPERIS* Stack

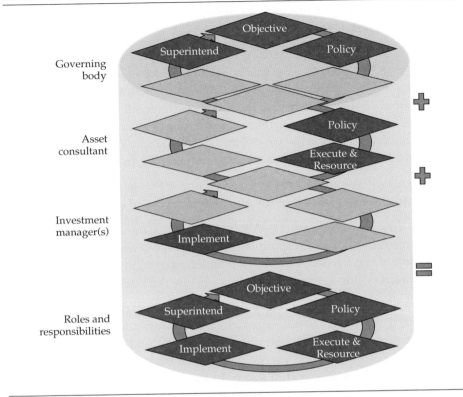

- *below the line (external)*—we have key service providers (say, the asset consultant(s), external investment managers, the actuary, administration, custody) undertake the exercise as well.

Each of these groups gathers for only 30 minutes (with this time allocation strictly enforced) in separate rooms. Each room has a large picture of the *OPERIS* framework (the five steps *and* detailed tasks within each step, some of which we have described throughout the book). Each group is armed with three colored sticky note pads—green, red, and yellow—and 20 blue dots:

- *Green means yes*—We undertake the specific task in the step.

- *Red means no*—We have no practical role in completing this task. In the case of the governing body, it may be that this role is operationally delegated.

- *Yellow means unsure*—We are not sure who is responsible for this task and want clarification.

- *Blue means priority*—Each group must place the number of blue dots against the tasks within each of the steps that they believe to be the most important that they undertake.

The rules are simple. All exercises must be run separately. Each group must assign a green (yes), red (no), or yellow (unsure) sticky note against *all* specific tasks within each of the five steps in the *OPERIS* framework. Each group must also allocate all 20 blue dots against those tasks within each step they deem most important. Following the completion of the exercise by the respective groups, we layer the results to create what we call an *OPERIS* stack. What are we looking for? What are the potential takeaways from the exercise? In summary:

- *Resourcing*—We are interested in which of the five steps (and tasks within each of these steps) the various groups prioritize and spend their time on.

- *Alignment* (or lack thereof)—We are particularly interested in testing the alignment of roles and responsibilities across the investment organization (in each of the five steps as well as broader subgroupings, say, those above the fiduciary line against those in roles below the fiduciary line).

- *Gaps and overlaps*—If any task within a step (or steps) does not have at least one party with a yellow or green sticky note against it, there might be a gap in the process and some uncertainty as to roles and responsibilities. The converse occurs when all parties put a green sticky note (and lots of blue dots) on, say, one task within a step. In this case, even though many *claim* responsibility, we question whether the *real* responsibility is very clear.

- *Ambiguity*—More yellow means more ambiguity. Through simple visualization, we are interested in the proportion of yellow (unsure) sticky notes across the groups. Are they clustered in the same steps or specific tasks within a step?

We share this outline of our *OPERIS* stack as a possible way for governing bodies to think about monitoring in a much broader way than perhaps undertaken traditionally. The *OPERIS* stack is our attempt to directly target, as stated at the start of this section, one of the most pressing challenges facing those who govern the investment process. Our anecdotal observations suggest that the very process of undertaking this exercise produces positive outcomes for the investment organization. It can be the catalyst for a shared framework for understanding and new opportunities for trust-based engagement for those above and below the fiduciary line.

We think of the *OPERIS* stack as being akin to using drone technology on a building site: perspectives are changed, and from those different perspectives, new insights are formed. Governing bodies that formally monitor roles and responsibilities are building an investment process by acknowledging a world in which outcomes are unknown and unknowable.

Mandate Compliance

We now move from the bigger picture of the *OPERIS* stack to the detail required to monitor investment restrictions and guidelines—what we consider mandate compliance.[134] Good governance requires the governing body to ensure, typically through delegation, daily investment compliance, including the monitoring of limits, restrictions, and investment guidelines sourced from key policy documents, such as the following:

- the IPS (see Chapter 5),

- investment management agreements (IMAs),[135]

- investment policies and guidelines,

- a derivative risk statement, and

- any investment-related policies that form part of the governing body's wider enterprise risk management system.

In our experience, mandate compliance has been, for very sound reasons, largely delegated. Governing bodies typically marshal resources to answer the question, are we doing things right? Mandate compliance–oriented tasks provide oversight and validation of the custodian, external investment managers, and, when applicable, the internal investment office on behalf of the fiduciary.[136] A host of industry-leading resources is available for those fiduciary

---

[134]We are focusing on the investment aspects of the compliance of delegates with their approved mandates. The matter of regulatory compliance is separate, and we return to it in Chapter 9.

[135]There will be IMAs with external investment managers (as standard) and, increasingly, IMAs with internal investment teams.

[136]Some of the major tasks undertaken by the compliance-oriented function include building and implementing systems of compliance that provide a clear, aligned, unambiguous, and consistent approach to the interpretation and monitoring of IMAs; delivery of accurate compliance monitoring reports; ensuring adherence to procedures and control checks; conducting trade compliance monitoring and reporting (external and internal); evaluating and monitoring key service providers; providing an investigative function when breaches of mandate occur and recommendations for improvement; and monitoring all organization settings (such as currency exposures, counterparty exposures, credit support annexures), and other compliance requirements (e.g., excluded securities) and relevant legislation (say, anti-money-laundering and counterterrorism financing). As fiduciary investors continue to source and appoint investment managers from around the world, an accompanying increase will be needed of governance resources to coordinate compliance activities internationally. Research in the field of financial geography may provide insights for such cross-border coordination; see Wojcik, Knight, and Pazitka (2017).

Exhibit 29.   Evidentiary Basis for Best Practice

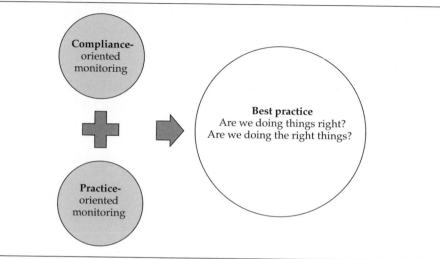

boards seeking to move their mandate compliance–oriented activities toward best practice.[137]

If the challenges facing those delegated by the governing body with mandate compliance were not substantial enough, best practice requires that fiduciary investors also engage in *practice-oriented monitoring* of investment activities. Practice-oriented monitoring seeks assurance that "we are doing the right things." Specifically, the question for the governing body is, are we doing the right things to achieve our investment outcomes? As **Exhibit 29** illustrates, we do not view compliance-oriented and practice-oriented monitoring as distinct domains. Quite the opposite, we see compliance-oriented monitoring as enabling practice-oriented monitoring. We believe that the governing body is providing an evidentiary basis for claiming best practice by undertaking both compliance- and practice-oriented monitoring.

Risk Assurance

In this book, we have largely confined our discussion to those risks most closely associated with investment governance and left a detailed discussion of noninvestment enterprise-wide risks to others.[138] We assume that the wider

---

[137]For an example, see State Street Global Services (2014) on the current and future challenges of compliance for asset owners.

[138]The various non-investment-related risk categories require careful governance by the fiduciary investor, of course, as they would in any other form of industrial organization. For further discussion about enterprise-wide risk management, see OECD (2014).

organization has identified, defined, evaluated, and prioritized all the risk categories that constitute its *enterprise-wide risk management* (ERM) system. Given the nature of the economic activity undertaken, a prioritization of risks based on, say, potential impact and likelihood would result in investment-related risks being ranked as one of the highest, if not the very highest, risk facing the fiduciary investor.[139] Therefore, the governing body would "own" (i.e., have accountability for) these investment-related risks and seek ongoing assurance of the management of such risks. It is vital that the governing body—and its delegates—incorporate its investment-related risk assurance activities in Step S of the *OPERIS* framework *within* the investment organization's broad ERM system. As noted in Chapter 1, just as there are as many investment issues as there are fiduciary investors, there is no "one-size-fits-all" solution to investment-related (and enterprise-wide) risk assurance.

To build an effective, independent investment-related risk management process, the governing body may delegate assurance responsibilities to a chief risk officer (CRO), or equivalent—a delegate who is becoming increasingly important in the fiduciary investor context. The CRO's role in defined-benefit (DB) plans, defined-contribution (DC) plans, and endowments and foundations (E&Fs) is critical in providing enterprise-wide (including investment-related) assurance and meeting the ever-increasing requirements of regulators. The CRO can also be delegated to help the governing body implement a "three lines of defense" model for the investment organization. **Exhibit 30** illustrates these three lines.

Readers who are familiar with the traditional "three lines of defense" framework will note that in our definition of the third line, we have explicitly

Exhibit 30. Three Lines of Defense

First line	Management controls and internal controls
Second line	Risk management, compliance, and specialist reports
Third line	Internal and external audit, regulators

---

[139]We strongly encourage fiduciary investors to formally develop an ERM system that includes the documenting of a risk assurance map.

included "external auditors" and "regulators."[140] The rationale for this decision, particularly in the context of financial institutions, is provided by Arndorfer and Minto (2015).

Although the CRO's role is critical, the governing body should *actively discourage* any perception that risk management tasks are only undertaken by the risk and compliance team (or, equivalent, reporting to the CRO). We encourage the fiduciary investor to formally enshrine that the CRO has a direct line to the governing body (or perhaps a direct line to the audit and risk committee). Risk and compliance hurdles should be formally embedded in the remuneration structures of investment-related staff (sometimes referred to as the "front office"). Furthermore, the remuneration of staff in the investment-related risk function "should not be linked to the performance of the activities it monitors" (Chiu 2015)—otherwise, the staff will tolerate too much risk in the hope of a big payoff.[141] This is particularly important for those delegated by the governing body to provide assurance regarding the performance of external *and* internal investment teams.

Good investment governance requires that assurance regarding the investment-related risks arising from Steps E&R and I of the *OPERIS* framework be an ongoing process. A topical debate for governing bodies in recent years is how "best" to apply the three lines of defense not only as related to enterprise-wide risks but also specifically to the investment-related risks faced by the fiduciary investor. Abbott and Devey (2017) argued that governing bodies should be more proactive and less reactive in their approach to risk assurance. This admonition is a valuable reminder for governing bodies that investment-related risks are *prospective* not retrospective. Risk assurance practices should not solely involve preparing for yesterday's financial crisis; more crises surely will come, but they most assuredly will not be exactly like the last one. The challenge in moving to a more proactive approach is that it requires the governing body to not only have clarity about risk tolerances (see the Davey 2015 model in Chapter 3), but also develop a higher-level statement related to its investment risk attitude—more commonly referred to as its "risk appetite."

Risk Appetite. According to ISO 31000:2009, risk appetite is defined as the "organization's approach to assess and eventually pursue, retain, take or turn away from risk."[142] In moving to best practice, governing bodies must practically ensure ongoing assurance regarding their *tolerance of* and *appetite*

---

[140]See the excellent work of the Institute of Internal Auditors (2013).
[141]Chiu (2015) noted, "U.K. legislation specifically provides the Chief Risk Officer's remuneration should be decided by the Board."
[142]See ISO 31000:2009: Risk management at www.iso.org/obp/ui/#iso:std:iso:31000:ed-1:v1:en.

for investment-related risks.[143] As discussed in Chapter 3, the governing body must have clarity regarding its "risk tolerance"—the tactical, operational framing of acceptable variations surrounding investment-related risks (Rittenberg and Martens 2012).

In our experience, governing bodies typically have defensible processes or standards regarding their investment-related risks. For example:

- *benchmark based*—benchmark plus 2%;

- *inflation based*—CPI plus 5%;

- *risk based*—expect a negative return, say, one in every five years; or

- *peer based*—we aim to beat the median peer group performance over rolling three-year periods.

In their own words ...

"A further cause of confusion is that in many funds the (unspoken) objective is peer relative returns, usually over a single year. So, the CIO's priority is relative returns. The problem is relative returns only represent a very small part of the real risk borne by default members. Should not the task of the most senior investment staff be to manage the bulk of the risk?"

—*Brad Holzberger, Chief Investment Officer, QSuper*

We strongly support governing bodies in seeking ongoing assurance of these important investment-related "risk tolerances." But what if the beneficiary's objective (see Chapter 3) is a little more nuanced and located more in the strategic domain? Consider the following investment-related outcomes that a beneficiary might be seeking:

- *DB plans*—Success may be defined as having sufficient assets to meet the present value of all future liabilities.

- *DC plans*—The beneficiaries may seek a proportion (say, 70%) of their preretirement income as a real-income stream over their retirement years.

- *E&Fs*—The board of an endowment fund may have to meet an agreed-on (or statutory) spending objective (say, 5% per year) to support a multiyear cancer research study.

---

[143]Investment risk appetite is defined by Pompian (2017) as the "willingness to take risk."

Investment-related risks framed in this way require the governing body to be (very) clear—particularly with those to whom responsibility is delegated—on how much investment-related risk the board is willing to take to "solve" the beneficiary's investment problem. From a practical perspective, the governing body might consider an investment-related risk "dashboard" (or similar mechanism) to formally oversee metrics related to their agreed-on risk tolerance and risk appetite on an ongoing basis.[144] For the governing body to seek assurance over investment objectives that are framed in a broader and more strategic domain, the governing body must articulate and oversee assurance of investment-related risks informed by documented risk appetite. Given the *OPERIS* framework discussion, the natural way of framing risk ought to be found in the investment objectives, captured in the HIO (Chapter 4). We would be most surprised to find an important investment-related risk measure not captured in the HIO.

A Final Word

In "closing the loop," the governing body must carry out its role as superintendent of the investment process. Our discussion regarding the final step of the *OPERIS* framework began with the governing body seeking assurance regarding the *alignment* of the chain of trusted relationships across the investment process, establishing the need for mandate compliance, and specifying an ongoing process that ensures that investment-related risk tolerance and risk appetite settings will be obeyed. Some readers may be surprised that we have dedicated a chapter to different ways of seeking alignment and assurance of risk management practices across the investment organization. We view those governing bodies that can move their investment organization to best practices in these areas as not only fulfilling their fiduciary duty to the beneficiary but also as creating a source of comparative advantage over other investors. Our observation from the field is that many "other" types of investors see step five in the *OPERIS* framework as little more than monthly performance reporting and largely operational investment-related reviews (compare the investment committee agenda of the hypothetical ABC Fund in Chapter 6). The world's leading fiduciary investors understand that the management of investment-related risks must be informed by (and aligned to) the beneficiary's investment challenge and the broader enterprise-wide risk settings. That is, "success" is to be evaluated

---

[144]For an enterprise-wide perspective on the ongoing monitoring of risk appetite, see Corbett (2017).

in terms of whether the investment objectives were achieved as part of a broader set of organizational objectives.

As introduced in Chapter 3, achieving investment outcomes for the beneficiary is *not*, in many instances, simply a function of investment returns. Outcomes can be driven by expected returns *and* a range of additional factors, including, to name but a few,

- cash flow profile,

- time horizon,

- interest rates (and what they mean for discount rates),

- price of inflation-hedging assets,

- longevity and tail of the liabilities, and

- risk aversion.[145]

To illustrate this idea, we will use the DC plan context during the global financial crisis (GFC) of 2007–2008. Imagine a scenario in which the governing body of a DC plan was formally reviewing its investment-related risks on 30 June 2009. The risk assessment report noted that "we were only down 19% during the GFC, when comparable DC plan peers fell 29%." Such an assessment takes a "peer-based" view of risk—the investment process worked (very) well when compared with comparable approaches (as one view of "risk tolerance"). Imagine a member of the same the DC plan reviewing her investment-related risks on the same date. Her "personal" risk assessment may have said something like, "I retired on 1 July 2009 and have started drawing on my retirement nest egg. Yikes, I experienced a 19% fall in my DC plan balance!" Our hypothetical DC plan beneficiary rightly takes a broader (and dimmer) view of "risk appetite" that includes other investment-related risks—for instance, the risk of *not* "replacing 70% of preretirement income" (Chapter 3).[146]

This discussion leads us neatly to the final tasks within the **S**uperintend step—namely, monitoring, reporting, and review. We consider these issues in Chapter 9.

---

[145]Wilkinson (2017) considered these specific issues in the context of DB plans.

[146]For further discussion of sequencing risk, see Basu and Drew (2009); Milevsky and Macqueen (2010); and Basu, Doran, and Drew (2012).

Points for Reflection: Chapter 8. Closing the Loop: Superintending Roles and Responsibilities

As a fiduciary:

- Am I clear about how to determine whether we are "on track" (or not) to achieving our investment objective? Can I say what would necessitate a midcourse change of direction and what evidence would be required?

- Can I explain, at a high level, the process for determining the likelihood of meeting the beneficiary's HIO?

- Am I involved in a regular process of monitoring how the governing body and its delegates are discharging their roles and responsibilities over time?

- Do I ensure an appropriate balance of resources dedicated to mandate compliance–oriented tasks ("are we doing things right?") and practice-oriented monitoring ("are we doing the right things?")? Can I point to an evidentiary basis for claiming best practices in both of these areas?

- Am I comfortable that the governing body clearly "owns" (i.e., has accountability for) investment-related risks and seeks ongoing assurance of the management of such risks across the organization?

- Can I explain how investment-related risks are placed within the ERM system to ensure ongoing assurance regarding the management of such risks?

- Does evidence support that risk management has the appropriate level of organizational visibility? Have I considered whether, as part of our enterprise-wide assurance, the appointment of a CRO is appropriate for the organization?

- Can I describe how the governing body uses the three lines of defense model in day-to-day risk assurance?

- Can I articulate, in simple terms, the governing body's risk appetite? Can I point to evidence about how our risk appetite is practically embedded in the investment process?

- Do I regularly consider an investment-related risk dashboard (or similar method), and can I describe how this dashboard is used in monitoring risks?

- Do I understand, and can I explain, the key drivers of success from an investment perspective? Do I have clarity on what we can and, perhaps more important, what we cannot control?

- Is my perception of risk peer based or beneficiary based? Can I provide an evidentiary basis for such a view?

9. Monitoring, Reporting, and Review

"Investment concepts are generally taught, learnt and spoken about among professionals in time-weighted terms. According to this view of the world, returns are the sole determinant of performance and risk, and a given return has an identical impact no matter its timing. We find that time-weighted measures overlook important aspects of retirement investing, whereas wealth-denominated, target-relative measures more accurately capture the dynamics of retirement investing. Thus, we see *the two faces of investment performance and risk*."

—*Bianchi, Drew, Evans, and Walk (2014)*

The final step in the *OPERIS* framework, **Superintend**, as shown in **Exhibit 31**, requires the governing body to ensure effective *monitoring, reporting*, and *review* of the investment process. The tasks undertaken as part of Step S are a component of the investment organization's process of risk management and assurance (see Chapter 8). Step S is critical for providing those serving above the fiduciary line with the transparency they need—disclosure,

Exhibit 31.   *OPERIS* Framework: Superintend, Part 2

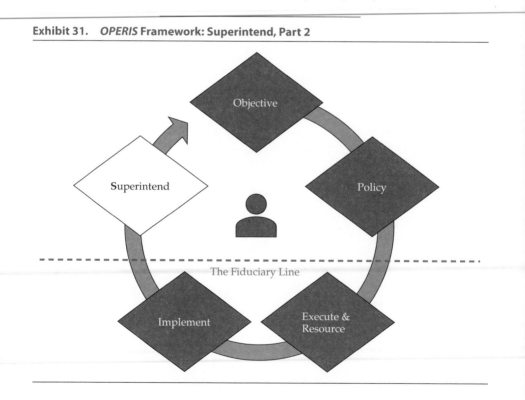

clarity, constancy, and accuracy—to evaluate activities throughout the investment process. The results should be documented and reported both internally and, as required, externally. Moreover, the results provide the evidence base on which the governing body can build a culture of continuous improvement across the investment process.

We make the case in this chapter for the governing body to take a *dual-focused* approach to monitoring. This approach acknowledges that activities undertaken below the fiduciary line—the performance of investment managers—are typically measured by time-weighted return metrics. In many instances, however, the beneficiary's investment objective—meeting a liability (defined-benefit [DB] plans), retirement adequacy (defined-contribution [DC] plans), and grant programs (endowments and foundations [E&Fs])—are money-weighted in nature. In this regard, dual-focused monitoring requires consideration of time- and money-weighted returns, estimation of the probability of achieving the investment objective, and multidimensional risk analysis. In this chapter, we specifically consider

- the two faces of performance and risk,

- escalating issues—what to do with red flags,

- reporting—who gets what, and

- review—the foundation of continuous improvement.

We again acknowledge that the topics we have selected are only a sampling of those that governing bodies can consider when deciding on their approach to monitoring, reporting, and review in Step S. We assume that the governing body is following CFA Institute Global Investment Performance Standards (GIPS®) to calculate and present investment results.[147] We also assume that the investment organization takes a structured approach to enterprise-wide risk management, such as the ISO 31000 international standard, and has also adopted ISO-like standards for the governing body, such as the Prudent Practices for Investment Stewards by fi360.[148] Similarly, we assume that the governing body has met its reporting and assessment responsibilities to regulators and additional requirements as, say, a signatory to the United Nations–supported Principles for Responsible Investment.[149] Finally, it is a

---

[147]For more on the GIPS® standards, see www.cfainstitute.org/ethics/codes/gipsstandards/Pages/index.aspx.

[148]For fi360's approach, see fi360, *Prudent Practices for Investment Stewards* (Pittsburgh: 2013). In the interests of full disclosure, both authors hold the designation of Accredited Investment Fiduciary Analyst® and are CEFEX Analysts (www.cefex.org/IndustryExpertise.aspx).

[149]For a discussion of PRI's standards, see, www.unpri.org/pri.

given that all the individuals involved across the investment organization follow the letter and spirit of their profession's code of ethics and professional standards.[150]

The Two Faces of Performance and Risk

Fiduciary investors have, as a core task, the responsibility of earning investment returns for their beneficiaries.[151] So, return-based performance and risk measures are of central concern to those above and below the line and, of course, the beneficiary. Although such measures will always have a place in investment governance, management, and communications, our motivation in this section is to consider whether a singular focus on these measures—which typically relate to inputs—obscures a more complete understanding of the investment objective.

As discussed previously, the beneficiary's investment objective—in our three contexts (DC plans, DB plans, and E&Fs)—are typically money-weighted in nature; that is, outcomes are a function of both returns *and* the amount of capital to which the return applies. For governing bodies, returns are but one—albeit an important—determinant of the investment outcome. Note the institutional setting in which the governing body operates. In, say, a DC plan context, retirement adequacy at an individual level becomes the objective of retirement savings. This reality shines a bright light on what's important for the beneficiary, the *individual* DC plan member, and the prescriptions it has for both the monitoring of DC plan performance (the focus of this chapter) and future investment strategy.

Given this circumstance, what is the most appropriate way to consider investment outcomes for governing bodies? We suggest that those above the fiduciary line develop a dual-focused approach to monitoring—a set of fiduciary analytics that can be used to evaluate both historical performance *and* expected future performance. We first introduced this idea of fiduciary analytics as part of the investment process discussed in Chapter 4. We can see from **Exhibit 32** that fiduciary analytics (Step 4) is an integral part of the process of evaluating competing asset allocations to achieve an HIO (Step 5). A poorly considered "battery of fiduciary analytics" may result in an incorrect inference about what constitutes "optimality" (as defined in Chapter 4).

---

[150]See the CFA Institute Code of Ethics and Standards of Professional Conduct at www.cfainstitute.org/ethics/codes/ethics/Pages/index.aspx.
[151]This discussion is based on our work with Robert J. Bianchi (Griffith University) and Michael Evans. See Bianchi, Drew, Evans, and Walk (2014) and Bianchi, Drew, and Walk (2013, 2014, 2016 [a and b]) for further discussion.

Exhibit 32. Fiduciary Analytics and the Investment Process

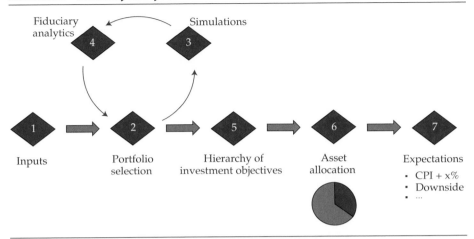

Recall from Chapter 4 that we use a battery of fiduciary analytics to measure and illustrate performance in a variety of ways, such as time-weighted and money-weighted measures (incorporating distributional properties, risk-adjusted performance measures, downside risk metrics, and visualization). We encourage governing bodies to use this same battery of analytics to create a three-dimensional view of performance to monitor those below the fiduciary line. Finally, we suggest to governing bodies that, given the use of fiduciary analytics in asset allocation *ex ante* (Step 4 of Exhibit 32), they also be used to evaluate performance *ex post* (Step 6 of Exhibit 32).

Following the same approach we used to discuss investment beliefs in Chapter 2, we outline our standard battery of fiduciary analytics, shown in **Exhibit 33**, as a starting point for consideration by the governing body. Our motivation is not to convince the reader that our approach is the final word on fiduciary analytics. This approach is our *standard* set of analytics; we tailor the monitoring metrics that would best align with the fiduciary's investment challenge. The process of ensuring consistency between the time- and money-weighted measures and the essence of the investment challenge is an order of magnitude more important than secondary debates about one specific metric over another.

A *dual-focused* approach to fiduciary analytics—the monitoring component of Step S of the *OPERIS* framework—can be likened to a global positioning system for the fiduciary investor. To use our aviation metaphor, where exactly are we in relation to the destination (where the destination is the set of investment objectives as they relate to the investment issue)? In our experience, such an approach to fiduciary analytics can provide evidence-based

Exhibit 33.   Dual-Focused Analytics

Time-Weighted Analytics	Money-Weighted Analytics
Mean	Median retirement wealth ratio
Standard deviation	Probability of shortfall
Sharpe ratio	Expected shortfall
Negative return 1-in-X years	Sortino ratio

Source: Bianchi, Drew, Evans, and Walk (2014).

insight into questions regarding time- and money-weighted performance issues:

- *Time-weighted perspectives*—As noted by Bacon (2004), performance measurement answers three basic questions: (1) "What" is the return on assets? (2) "Why" has the portfolio performed that way? (3) "How" can we improve performance? Work on the practice of performance measurement and attribution is voluminous, but we particularly note the many contributions by William F. Sharpe (1966)[152] of Stanford University, Martin J. Gruber (1996) of New York University, and Russell Wermers (2000) of the University of Maryland. We also recommend works by practitioners such as Carl Bacon (2004), François-Serge Lhabitant (2004, 2017), and David Spaulding (1997, 2003).

- *Money-weighted perspectives*—We incorporate the distributional properties, risk-adjusted money-weighted performance measures, and downside risk metrics. Note the work of Philippe Jorion (2007), Philip Booth (1997),[153] and Frank A. Sortino (2010).[154] Again, this is not a complete catalog of resources for governing bodies, but it is a starting point to consider evaluating past performance and the likelihood of achieving future investment outcomes.

The fiduciary reader may wonder where all the detail is. As noted, the numerous excellent resources about performance evaluation can be consulted *once* the governing body has reflected on the investment challenge it faces and how it proposes to evaluate and monitor performance. The risk of adding the details at this point would be that this book stops being one about

---

[152]Sharpe's contributions to the field earned him a share in the 1990 Sveriges Riksbank Prize in Economic Sciences in Memory of Alfred Nobel, commonly referred to as "the Nobel Prize in Economics."

[153]For an actuarial perspective on risk, also see Clarkson (1989) and Booth and Yakoubov (2000).

[154]Also see Sortino and Price (1994).

investment governance for fiduciaries and becomes an instruction manual on performance evaluation that would, appropriately, be filled with equations. Modestly, we hope that we have given the fiduciary some things to think about when the governing body next meets.

In their own words …

"Strong investment governance allows fiduciaries to make decisions, assess investments and monitor performance against well-structured and relevant criteria."

—*Danielle Press, Commissioner,*
Australian Securities and Investments Commission

Escalating Issues—What to Do with Red Flags

The **S**uperintend step in the *OPERIS* framework requires the governing body to provide evidence that monitoring, reporting, and review are undertaken to meet the highest standards. Whereas we engaged with some of the challenges of monitoring in Step I by suggesting the use of dual-focused fiduciary analytics, we now turn to matters related to reporting and review. In the wake of the Bernie Madoff scandal, criminology and finance scholars have revisited the important role of enterprise-wide risk *reporting*—particularly the role of reporting red flags in a wider system of internal and external controls.[155,156] Capital market history suggests that the stronger the investment returns, the weaker investor and regulator vigilance becomes, with vigilance returning only when the party is over (Jickling 2009).

Red flags (or anomalies) are a set of circumstances that are unusual in nature or vary from the normal activity. They are a signal that something out of the ordinary has occurred (or is occurring) and may need further investigation (Grabosky and Duffield 2001). A deep dive into the mechanics of red-flag systems as part of a broader assurance system is beyond the scope of this book. To readers with an interest in this important topic, we recommend the work of Cressey (1953) on the social psychology of embezzlement (and the fraud triangle). We encourage governing bodies to exhibit an "anxious

---

[155]The discussion of red flags, Ponzi schemes, and white-collar crime is based on our research collaboration led by Jacqueline M. Drew, Griffith University; see Drew and Drew (2010a, 2010b, 2012).
[156]Gregoriou and Lhabitant (2009) described the Madoff case as a "flock of red flags."

vigilance" (Smith [1776] 1937) when identifying, escalating, and acting on red flags across the investment organization. We envision delegating the daily responsibility for this issue to the chief risk officer.[157]

Perhaps the bigger issue related to the escalation of red flags across the investment organization is the problem of hindsight bias. As noted by Gregoriou and Lhabitant (2009) and Drew and Drew (2010a), the (many) red flags associated with the Madoff case seem alarmingly obvious "in hindsight." The challenge for the governing body when designing fraud detection systems relates directly to this most critical of features—overcoming hindsight bias. Fischhoff's (1975) seminal work on the effect of outcome knowledge on judgment under conditions of uncertainty is important in this regard. Fischhoff, supported by subsequent studies, suggested that hindsight bias is hardwired into the human condition.[158] Fiduciary investors need to apply a multidimensional approach—proactive and preventative—to risk detection, acknowledging the complementarity of internal and external controls (Drew and Drew 2010b).[159]

Reporting—Who Gets What

Fiduciary investors have a duty of care to keep written financial and investment records. Assuming the governing body has ensured its ongoing fulfillment of duties under general law and statutory obligations, the issue we seek to briefly explore in this section is the role of reporting—specifically, who gets what, how often do they get it, and most important, what are the effects of such decisions? Ultimately, this set of questions reduces to one challenge: ensuring the consistency of the governance budget with the investment governance settings and the nature of the investment challenge. For example, we despair at the low priority placed on what we believe to be such high-value-added functions like a secretariat that ensures that meetings are arranged, invitations are sent, and governing body papers are delivered so that fiduciaries have the time necessary to deliberate on their contents before the meeting. The risk is that the governing body—and those who support it—will

---

[157]For those readers seeking further discussion, see Baldwin and Cave (1998).

[158]We can, sadly, recall the various investigations into the 9/11 terror attacks, or more recently, the subprime lending crisis, the collapse of Lehman Brothers, and the long list of red flags that were supposedly clearly evident in the lead-up to those events (Drew and Drew 2010b). As Daniel Kahneman, awarded the Nobel Memorial Prize in Economics Sciences in 2002, observed, "hindsight bias makes surprises vanish."

[159]Some literature also considers the role of financial literacy levels and fraud victimization, see Drew (2013) and Drew and Cross (2013).

focus not on what might be described as "good administration" but on "the shiny new concept" they read about in yesterday's trade press.

With the award of the 2017 Nobel Prize in Economics to behavioral economist Richard Thaler of the University of Chicago, we are reminded of the importance of human behavior in economic decision making. For example, the work of Kraft, Vashishtha, and Venkatachalam (2018) has reignited the myopia debate regarding the quarterly reporting requirement for corporations in the United States. Specifically, Kraft et al. (2018) found that increased reporting frequency is associated with an economically large *decline* in investments made by corporations. Although the debate regarding myopia will continue in scholarly, practitioner, and regulator circles, it is important that the governing body provide the investment organization with clarity on *who* gets *what* reporting and *when*. Acknowledging that formal reporting on myopia-related issues can be both complex and multidimensional, we suspect that the governing body will seek assurance regarding, for example,

- the corporate governance preferences of fiduciary investors and the impact on returns (McCahery, Sautner, and Starks 2016),

- the ability to check for myopia in the mandates issued by the fiduciary investor (Drew 2009),

- *myopic loss aversion* by investment managers (Eriksen and Kvaløy 2010; Benartzi and Thaler 1995), and

- myopia exhibited by the companies in which the governing body invests (Stein 1989).

We could devote a whole chapter to each of these issues; the difficulty of the task is not a reason that it should be ignored by the governing body. Each of these matters is worthy of formal reporting and consideration by the governing body and can be used to improve the investment process in the future.

Review—The Foundation of Continuous Improvement

As we come to the end of the *OPERIS* framework, Step S, Parts 1 and 2, we see the process of formal review as evidence of good practice. It is an opportunity for the governing body to evaluate the various strategic settings made in Steps O (Chapters 2 and 3) and P (Chapters 4 and 5) and their implementation in Steps E&R (Chapter 6) and I (Chapter 7). It also provides a regular review of the efficacy and conviction with which investment beliefs are held (Chapter 2). This review process allows the governing body to formally consider—and prioritize—prevailing endogenous and exogenous challenges facing the investment organization. Most important, marginal decisions that may result from the ongoing review process can be considered in light of the HIO (Chapter 4).

We are reminded of Tilles's (1963) remarks about how to evaluate corporate strategy, "No good military officer would undertake even a small-scale attack on a limited objective without a clear concept of his (her) strategy." The work by Tilles is relevant in the fiduciary context because it reminds governing bodies of the need to formally review the investment process in light of the beneficiary's investment objective, including internal and external consistency, the appropriateness of strategy given the level of resourcing (governance budget), risk tolerance and risk appetite of the governing body, precision in defining decision rights, time horizon, and alignment. Tilles's work largely focused on the qualitative aspects of a strategic review; we also encourage governing bodies to complement this analysis with quantitative evidence, including an agreed-on battery of fiduciary analytics as first introduced in Chapter 4. We expect that any decisions made as a result of the review be documented in the investment policy statement (Chapter 5) and the settings contained in it (e.g., the fee budget, risk budget).[160]

In our experience, Step S of the *OPERIS* framework is often considered an "administrative necessity" rather than a source of comparative advantage over other investors. We contend that this step can align the investment process, provide ongoing assurance, *and* develop an evidence base for the marginal decision by the governing body.

A Final Word

Finally, we recommend that the governing body *Superintend*—specifically, monitor—the investment-related communications of the fiduciary investor to gain assurance that the beliefs "are lived" across the investment organization. Our argument is that "alignment" is about both policy and behavior.[161]

Take the case of a governing body whose investment objective is, say, meeting the liabilities of a DB plan 30 years in the future. If the executives who act on behalf of the fiduciary sound like media commentators who opine on day-to-day movements in markets or boast that "we beat peers over the past year," they are not behaving in accordance with the principles discussed in this book. If the discussion focuses on, say, the extent to which the fiduciary

---

[160]We suggest that governing bodies ensure that foundational governance documents, such as the IPS, be controlled in a manner consistent with ISO 9001:2015.

[161]We first indicated how the *OPERIS* framework can assist in framing communications—in relation to investment objectives—in Chapter 3.

is on track to meet liabilities in 2049 or how the funding ratio of the plan is improving, that approach is a different and much better story. Such framing is clearly aligned with the investment objective of the beneficiary.

We raise this issue within the context of Step S because the governing body seeks to superintend the investment process *in its entirety*—including how the investment organization frames its communications with beneficiaries. If the governing body—and its delegates—are in the "public square" engaged in a running commentary on, say, daily market action, the same governing body should not be surprised when beneficiaries also make decisions that are short term in nature (Drew 2009).

Points for Reflection: Chapter 9. Monitoring, Reporting, and Review

As a fiduciary:

- Do I ensure that the governing body allocates appropriate governance time to consider both time- and money-weighted performance metrics?

- Can I explain, at a high level, why this dual-focused approach is critical to achieving objectives?

- Can I point to an agreed-on (and documented) set of fiduciary analytics that evaluates both historical performance and expected future performance?

- Am I able to point to evidence as to why our particular set of performance metrics has been selected to monitor performance?

- Can I describe how we use dual-focused analytics to ensure that we address the investment problem we seek to solve?

- Given our approach to performance monitoring and risk controls, do I understand the actions that will result if certain predetermined thresholds are breached?

- Am I conscious of the role that myopia may play across the investment organization? Do I seek assurance regarding the impact of myopia on matters such as mandate design, investment manager behavior, and our corporate governance policies?

- Can I attest that, as an investment organization, we are authentic in our communication to beneficiaries and external stakeholders?

- Is my private and public discourse on investment matters aligned with our investment beliefs?

- Can I confidently say that we are consistent in the way we frame the investment issue throughout the investment organization?

Postscript

By now, we hope the reader agrees that the individual fiduciary and the governing body to which the fiduciary is appointed both face a difficult task. How does one faithfully represent the interests of beneficiaries when making complex investment decisions in the presence of uncertainty and competing interests? We argue that the best that can be hoped for, in the context of complexity and uncertainty, is a high *probability* of success. We humbly submit that anyone who thinks differently ought to walk a mile in the shoes of a "real-life" fiduciary.

In this book, we provided fiduciaries with some ideas that raise the probability of success. Almost all our suggestions have revolved around *good process*. It is through a defensible, repeatable, and documented process that fiduciaries give *evidence* of their efforts to serve beneficiaries and manage complexity and uncertainty. After those efforts have been made, the outcomes are what they are, and fiduciaries respond through a process of continuous improvement aimed at reaching the destination.

In making the case for good process, we shared with the reader a high-level outline of the process we use when consulting and counseling our fiduciary clients. We find that this process provides a nearly universal blueprint—noting that the investment challenge, and the investment policy statement that flows from it, can vary widely among, say, pension funds, endowments, and ultra-high-net-worth individuals—for addressing the issues all investors face. We emphasize one last time that we are *not* selling our process as the only possible path to success (or, at least, defensible fiduciary practice). We assert that having *a* process is more important than having *this* process.

A book about investment governance for fiduciaries is important because the task they face is of increasing importance the world over. Fiduciaries are trusted with being stewards of *other people's money*, money that has been set aside for important societal purposes, be that the retirement savings of thousands of workers, the wealth of nations, or the legacy and good works of a charity. We trust that this book makes a modest contribution to raising the standards of fiduciary practice.

References

Abbott, J., and C. Devey. 2017. *The Three Lines of Offense: When Uncertainty Is the Only Certainty, Is It Time for Companies to View Risk Management as a Competitive Advantage?* EY Insights (May). www.ey.com/Publication/vwLU-Assets/ey-three-lines-of-offense/$FILE/ey-three-lines-of-offense.pdf.

Aikin, B. 2017. "Who Is a Fiduciary and What Does a Fiduciary Investment Advisor Do?" Investments & Wealth Monitor (September/October): 24–28.

AIST. 2016. *Investment Manager Operational Due Diligence.* Australian Institute of Superannuation Trustees. AIST Guidance Note (June). www.aist.asn.au/media/837834/aist_odd_guidance_note_9_sept_2016.pdf.

Ambachtsheer, K. 2007. *Pension Revolution: A Solution to the Pensions Crisis.* New York: Wiley.

———. 2014. "The Case for Long-Termism." *Rotman International Journal of Pension Management* 7 (2): 6–15.

———. 2016. *The Future of Pension Management.* New York: Wiley.

Ambachtsheer, K., and D. Ezra. 2007. *Pension Fund Excellence.* New York: Wiley.

Amenc, Noël, F. Blanc-Brude, A. Chreng, and C. Tran. 2017. "The Rise of 'Fake Infra'." EDHEC Infrastructure Institute.

Ankrim, E., and C. Hensel. 1993. "Commodities in Asset Allocation: A Real Asset Alternative to Real Estate?" *Financial Analysts Journal* 49 (3): 20–29.

Arndorfer, I., and A. Minto. 2015. *The Four Lines of Defence Model for Financial Institutions.* BIS Occasional Paper 11 (December). www.bis.org/fsi/fsipapers11.pdf.

Arnott, R., V. Kalesnik, and L. Wu. 2017. *The Folly of Hiring Winners and Firing Losers, Part III of Alice in Factorland.* Research Affiliates Fundamentals (September). www.researchaffiliates.com/content/dam/ra/documents/630%20The%20Folly%20of%20Hiring%20Winners%20and%20Firing%20Losers.pdf.

APRA. 2013a. *Prudential Standard SPS 530: Investment Governance.* Australian Prudential Regulation Authority (July). www.apra.gov.au/Super/PrudentialFramework/Documents/Final-SPS-530-Investment-Governance-July-2013.pdf.

———. 2013b. *Prudential Standard SPS 521: Conflicts of Interest*. Australian Prudential Regulation Authority (July). www.apra.gov.au/Super/PrudentialFramework/Documents/Final-SPS-521-Conflicts-of-Interest-July-2013.pdf.

Australian Securities and Investments Commission. 2017. "Self-Managed Super Fund (SMSF)." Money Smart (20 June). www.moneysmart.gov.au/superannuation-and-retirement/self-managed-super-fund-smsf.

Bacon, K. 2004. *Practical Portfolio Performance Measurement and Attribution*. Hoboken, NJ: Wiley.

Badaoui, S., R. Deguest, L. Martellini, and V. Milhau. 2014. "Dynamic Liability-Driven Investing Strategies: The Emergence of a New Investment Paradigm for Pension Funds." Research paper. EDHEC Business School.

Bailey, J., and T. Richards. 2017. *A Primer for Investment Trustees: Understanding Investment Committee Responsibilities*. Charlottesville, VA: CFA Institute Research Foundation.

Baker, A., D. Logue, and J. Rader. 2004. *Managing Pension and Retirement Plans: A Guide for Employers, Administrators, and Other Fiduciaries*. Oxford, UK: Oxford University Press.

Baldwin, R., and M. Cave. 1999. *Understanding Regulation: Theory, Strategy and Practice*. Oxford, UK: Oxford University Press.

Basu, A., and M. Drew. 2009. "Portfolio Size and Lifecycle Asset Allocation in Pension Funds." *Journal of Portfolio Management* 35 (3): 61–72.

———. 2010. "The Appropriateness of Default Investment Options in Defined Contribution Plans: Australian Evidence." *Pacific-Basin Finance Journal* 18 (3): 290–305.

———. 2015. "The Value of Tail Risk Hedging in Defined Contribution Plans: What Does History Tell Us." *Journal of Pension Economics and Finance* 14 (3): 240–265.

Basu, A., A. Byrne, and M. Drew. 2011. "Dynamic Lifecycle Strategies for Target Date Retirement Funds." *Journal of Portfolio Management* 37 (2): 83–96.

Basu, A., B. Doran, and M. Drew. 2013. "Sequencing Risk: The Worst Returns in Their Worst Order." *JASSA: The Finsia Journal of Applied Finance* 43 (4): 7–13.

Bauer, R., and J. Dahlquist. 2001. "Market Timing and Roulette Wheels." *Financial Analysts Journal* 57 (1): 28–40.

Benartzi, S., and R. Thaler. 1995. "Myopic Loss Aversion and the Equity Premium Puzzle." *Quarterly Journal of Economics* 110 (1): 73–92.

Bender, J., R. Briand, D. Melas, and R. Subramanian. 2013. *Foundations of Factor Investing*. MSCI Research Insight (December). https://ssrn.com/abstract=2543990.

Bernanke, B. 2010. *Implications of the Financial Crisis for Economics*. Speech presented at the Conference Co-sponsored by the Center for Economic Policy Studies and the Bendheim Center for Finance, Princeton University, Princeton, NJ (24 September). www.federalreserve.gov/newsevents/speech/bernanke20100924a.htm.

Bianchi, R. 2010. "Principal and Agent Problems in Australian Responsible Entities." *Deakin Business Review* 3 (1): 24–31.

Bianchi, R., and M. Drew. 2010. "Hedge Funds, Regulation and Systemic Risk." *Griffith Law Review* 19 (1): 5–27.

Bianchi, R., M. Drew, and J. Fan. 2015. "Combining Momentum with Reversal in Commodity Futures." *Journal of Banking & Finance* 59: 423–444.

———. 2016. "Commodities Momentum: A Behavioral Perspective." *Journal of Banking & Finance* 72: 133–150.

Bianchi, R., M. Drew, and S. Pappas. 2017. "The Predictability of Risk-Factor Returns." In *Factor Investing: From Traditional to Alternative Risk Premia*, ed. E. Jurczenko, 99–126. London, UK: ISTE Press–Elsevier.

Bianchi, R., M. Drew, and A. Walk. 2013. "The Time Diversification Puzzle: Why Trustees Should Care." *JASSA: The Finsia Journal of Applied Finance* 43 (1): 51–55.

———. 2014. "Time Diversification and Contributions." *Academy of Taiwan Business Management Review* 10 (3): 75–83.

———. 2016a. "The Equity Risk Premium in Australia (1900–2014)." *Financial Planning Research Journal* 2 (1): 80–99.

———. 2016b. "The Time Diversification Puzzle: A Survey." *Financial Planning Research Journal* 2 (2): 12–48.

Bianchi, R., M. Drew, and T. Whittaker. 2017. *Is Listed Infrastructure a Fake Asset Class? An Asset Pricing Approach*. EDHEC Working Paper (July). http://edhec.infrastructure.institute/wp-content/uploads/publications/bianchi_whittaker2017_wp.pdf.

Bianchi, R., G. Bornholt, M. Drew, and M. Howard. 2014. "Long-Term U.S. Infrastructure Returns and Portfolio Selection." *Journal of Banking & Finance* 42: 314–325.

Bianchi, R., M. Drew, M. Evans, and A. Walk. 2014. "The Two Faces of Investment Performance and Risk." *JASSA: The Finsia Journal of Applied Finance* 44 (1): 6–12.

Blake, D. 1995. *Pension Schemes and Pension Funds in the United Kingdom*. Oxford, UK: Oxford University Press.

Blake, D., A. Cairns, and K. Dowd. 2009. "Designing a Defined-Contribution Plan: What to Learn from Aircraft Designers." *Financial Analysts Journal* 65 (1): 37–42.

Blanc-Brude, F., T. Whittaker, and S. Wilde. 2017. *Searching for a Listed Infrastructure Asset Class*. EDHEC Working Paper (June). http://edhec.infra-structure.institute/wp-content/uploads/publications/blanc-brude2016c.pdf.

Bodie, Z., R. Merton, and W. Samuelson. 1992. "Labor Supply Flexibility and Portfolio Choice in a Life Cycle Model." *Journal of Economic Dynamics & Control* 16 (3–4): 427–449.

Boone, N., and L. Lubitz. 2004. *Creating an Investment Policy Statement: Guidelines and Templates*. San Francisco, CA: FPA Press.

Booth, P. 1997. *The Analysis of Actuarial Investment Risk*. Actuarial Research Paper No. 93. London, UK: City University, London.

Booth, P., and Y. Yakoubov. 2000. "Investment Policy for Defined-Contribution Pension Scheme Members Close to Retirement: An Analysis of the 'Lifestyle' Concept." *North American Actuarial Journal (NAAJ)* 4 (2): 1–19.

Bower, J., and L. Paine. 2017. "The Error at the Heart of Corporate Leadership." *Harvard Business Review* 95 (3): 50–60.

Brakke, T. 2016. "Rethinking Due Diligence and Manager Selection." *CFA Institute Conference Proceedings Quarterly* 33 (2): 10–16.

Brinson, G., L. Hood, and G. Beebower. 1986. "Determinants of Portfolio Performance." *Financial Analysts Journal* 42 (4): 39–44.

Brown, S., and W. Goetzmann. 1995. "Performance Persistence." *Journal of Finance* 50 (2): 679–698.

Caesar, J. *The Gallic Wars*. Translated by W.A. McDevitte and W.S. Bohn

CalPERS. 2016. *CalPERS at a Glance.* California Public Employees' Retirement System. (30 June). www.calpers.ca.gov/docs/forms-publications/calpers-at-a-glance.pdf.

———. 2017a. *Review of Survey Results on Board Investment Consultants.* California Public Employees' Retirement System. (14 August). www.calpers.ca.gov/docs/board-agendas/201708/invest/item07a-00.pdf.

———. 2017b. *Board Consultant Review & Evaluation Project Results—FY2016–17.* California Public Employees' Retirement System. (14 August) www.calpers.ca.gov/docs/board-agendas/201708/invest/item07a-01.pdf.

———. 2017c. "Total Fund." *Investment Policy* 17 (April).

Callan Associates. 2017. 2017 Defined Contribution Trends: 10th Anniversary Edition (7 April). https://www.callan.com/wp-content/uploads/2017/01/Callan-2017-DC-Survey.pdf.

Carhart, M. 1997. "On Persistence in Mutual Fund Performance." *Journal of Finance* 52 (1): 57–82.

CBOE. 2017. CBOE Volatility Index® (VIX®). Chicago Board Options Exchange (6 October). www.cboe.com/products/vix-index-volatility/vix-options-and-futures/vix-index.

CFA Society of the UK. 2013. *Conflicts of Interest.* Position Paper (April). https://secure.cfauk.org/assets/3769/CFA1192_Conflict_Interest_Position_paper_v2.pdf.

Chilton, B. 2011. *Ponzimonium: How Scam Artists Are Ripping Off America.* New York: Commodity Futures Trading Commission.

Chiu, I. 2015. *Regulating (from) the Inside: The Legal Framework for Internal Control in Banks and Financial Institutions.* London, UK: Hart Publishing.

Chung, J., and D. Lim. 2017. "Harvard Endowment Chief Pushed for Steeper Devaluation of Assets." *Wall Street Journal* (15 December). www.wsj.com/articles/harvard-endowment-chief-pushed-for-steeper-devaluation-of-assets-1513252800

Clare, A., and C. Wagstaff. 2011. "Manager Selection: How Do You Choose a Good Fund Manager?" In *The Trustee Guide to Investment*, ed. A. Clare and C. Wagstaff. London: Palgrave Macmillan.

Clark, G. 1993. *Pensions and Corporate Restructuring in American Industry: A Crisis of Regulation.* Baltimore, MD: Johns Hopkins University Press.

———. 2000. *Pension Fund Capitalism*. Oxford, UK: Oxford University Press.

———. 2003. *European Pensions and Global Finance*. Oxford, UK: Oxford University Press.

———. 2012. "From Corporatism to Public Utilities: Workplace Pensions in the 21st Century." *Geographical Research* 50 (1): 31–46.

———. 2017. "The Financial Legacy of Pension Fund Capitalism." In *Handbook on the Geographies of Money and Finance*, ed. R. Martin and J. Pollard, 348–374. London, UK: Edward Elgar Publishing.

Clark, G., and A. Monk. 2014. "The Geography of Investment Management Contracts: The UK, Europe, and the Global Financial Services Industry." *Environment & Planning A* 46 (3): 531–549.

———. 2015. *The Contested Role of Investment Consultants: Ambiguity, Contract, and Innovation in Financial Institutions*. Working Paper (June).

———. 2017. *Institutional Investors in Global Markets*. Oxford, UK: Oxford University Press.

Clark, G., and R. Urwin. 2008. "Best-Practice Pension Fund Governance." *Journal of Asset Management* 9 (1): 2–21.

———. 2010. "Innovative Models of Pension Fund Governance in the Context of the Global Financial Crisis." *Pensions: An International Journal* 15 (1): 62–77.

Clark, G., A. Munnell, and M. Orszag, eds. 2006. *Oxford Handbook of Pensions and Retirement Income*. Oxford, UK: Oxford University Press.

Clarkson, R. 1989. "The Measurement of Investment Risk." *Journal of the Institute of Actuaries* 116 (1): 127–178.

CNBC. 2016. U.S. State Public Pension Unfunded Liabilities to Hit $1.75 trillion: Moody's. Staff Reporter, CNBC.com (7 October). www.cnbc.com/2016/10/07/us-state-public-pension-unfunded-liabilities-to-hit-175-trillion-moodys.html.

Cochrane, J. 2011. "Presidential Address: Discount Rates." *Journal of Finance* 66 (4): 1047–1108.

Collins, J. 2001. *Good to Great: Why Some Companies Make the Leap . . . and Others Don't*. New York: HarperCollins.

Commonwealth Bank of Australia. 2016. *Record Passengers on Sydney-Melbourne Route.* Economic Insights (23 March). www.commsec.com.au/content/dam/EN/ResearchNews/ECO_Insights_230316.pdf.

Corbett, M. 2017. What is the director's role in evaluating an organisation's risk appetite? Australian Institute of Company Directors. https://aicd.companydirectors.com.au/membership/membership-update/what-is-the-directors-role-in-evaluating-an-organisations-risk-appetite.

Cressey, D. 1953. *Other People's Money: A Study in the Social Psychology of Embezzlement.* Glencoe, IL: Free Press.

Cresswell, J. 2010. *Oxford Dictionary of Word Origins.* New York: Oxford University Press.

Davey, G. 2012. *On the Stability of Risk Tolerance.* FinaMetrica (June). www.riskprofiling.com/WWW_RISKP/media/RiskProfiling/Downloads/On_the_Stability_of_Risk_Tolerance.pdf.

———. 2015. "Getting Risk Right." *Investments & Wealth Monitor,* 33–39.

DiBruno, R. 2013. *How to Write an Investment Policy Statement.* Hoboken, NJ: Wiley.

Drew, J. 2013. "Cold, Warm, Warmer, Hot! Locating Financial Literacy Hot Spots." *Journal of Financial Services Marketing* 18 (3): 220–226.

Drew, J., and C. Cross. 2013. "Fraud and Its PREY: Conceptualising Social Engineering Tactics and Its Impact on Financial Literacy Outcomes." *Journal of Financial Services Marketing* 18 (3): 188–198.

Drew, J., and M. Drew. 2010a. "The Identification of Ponzi Schemes: Can a Picture Tell a Thousand Frauds?" *Griffith Law Review* 19 (1): 48–66.

———. 2010b. "Ponzimonium: Madoff and the Red Flags of Fraud." *Deakin Business Review* 3 (1): 5–17.

———. 2012. "Who Was Swimming Naked When the Tide Went Out? Introducing Criminology to the Finance Curriculum." *Journal of Business Ethics Education* 9 (2): 63–76.

Drew, M. 2006. "Superannuation: Switching and Roulette Wheels." *Australian Accounting Review* 16 (40): 22–31.

———. 2009. "The Puzzle of Financial Reporting and Corporate Short-Termism: A Universal Ownership Perspective." *Australian Accounting Review* 19 (4): 295–302.

Drew, M., and J. Stanford. 2003. "Returns from Investing in Australian Equity Superannuation Funds, 1991 to 1999." *Service Industries Journal* 23 (3): 74–84.

Drew, M., and A. Walk. 2015. "Just How Safe Are 'Safe Withdrawal Rates' in Retirement?" *Financial Planning Research Journal* 1 (1): 22–32.

―――. 2016. "Governance: The Sine Qua Non of Retirement Security." *Journal of Retirement* 4 (1): 19–28.

Drew, M., A. Walk, and J. West. 2015. "Conditional Allocations to Real Estate: An Antidote to Sequencing Risk in Defined Contribution Retirement Plans." *Journal of Portfolio Management* 41 (6): 82–95.

―――. 2015. *The Role of Asset Allocation in Navigating the Retirement Risk Zone*. Finsia (Financial Services Institute of Australasia) White Paper (April). http://finsia.com/docs/default-source/industry-reports-retirement-risk-zone/the-role-of-asset-allocation-in-navigating-the-retirement-risk-zone.pdf?sfvrsn=4\.

Drew, M., P. Stoltz, A. Walk, and J. West. 2014. "Retirement Adequacy through Higher Contributions: Is This the Only Way?" *Journal of Retirement* 1 (4): 57–74.

Earley, P. Christopher, and Elaine Mosakowski. 2000. "Creating Hybrid Team Cultures: An Empirical Test of Transnational Team Functioning." *Academy of Management Journal* 43 (1): 26–49.

Elder, Daniel. 2016. "Dealing with Market Volatility." *News Hub* (July). Qsuper. https://qsuper.qld.gov.au/News-Hub/Articles/2016/09/02/10/25/Dealing-with-Market-Volatility.

Ellis, C. 2011. "The Winners' Game." *Financial Analysts Journal* 67 (4): 11–17.

―――. 2013. *Winning the Loser's Game: Timeless Strategies for Successful Investing*, 6th ed. New York: McGraw-Hill.

―――. 2016. *The Index Revolution: Why Investors Should Join It Now*. New York: Wiley.

Ellis, C., A. Eschtruth, and A. Munnell. 2014. *Falling Short: The Coming Retirement Crisis and What to Do about It*. Oxford, UK: Oxford University Press.

"An Emerging Challenge." 2010. Schumpeter Blog. *Economist* (15 April). www.economist.com/node/15906206.

Eriksen, K., and O. Kvaløy. 2010. "Myopic Investment Management." *Review of Finance* 14 (3): 521–542.

Fama, E. 1965. "The Behavior of Stock-Market Prices." *Journal of Business* 38 (1): 34–105.

Feng, G., S. Giglio, and D. Xiu. 2017. *Taming the Factor Zoo.* Chicago Booth Research Paper No. 17-04 (August). https://ssrn.com/abstract=2934020.

fi360. 2016. *Prudent Practices for Investment Stewards.* Pittsburgh, PA: fi360.

FCA. 2017. *Asset Management Market Study*: Final Report. Financial Conduct Authority (June). www.fca.org.uk/publication/market-studies/ms15-2-3.pdf.

Finkenzeller, K., T. Dechant, and W. Schafers. 2010. "Infrastructure: A New Dimension of Real Estate? An Asset Allocation Analysis." *Journal of Property Investment & Finance* 28 (4): 263–274.

Fischhoff, B. 1975. "Hindsight Is Not Equal to Foresight: The Effect of Outcome Knowledge on Judgment under Uncertainty." *Journal of Experimental Psychology. Human Perception and Performance* 1 (3): 288–299.

Frankfurter, G., and H. Phillips. 1994. "A Brief History of MPT: From a Normative Model to Event Studies." *Journal of Investing* 3 (4): 18–23.

Fraser-Sampson, G. 2010. *Private Equity as an Asset Class*, 2nd ed. New York: Wiley.

Gallo, A. 2012. "Why Aren't You Delegating?" *Harvard Business Review* 26 (July). https://hbr.org/2012/07/why-arent-you-delegating.

Guardians of the New Zealand Super Fund. 2017. *Delegations.* Delegations Policy, version 13A (7 December). www.nzsuperfund.co.nz/nz-super-fund-explained-purpose-and-mandate/delegations.

Gigerenzer, G. 2008. "Why Heuristics Work." *Perspectives on Psychological Science* 3 (1): 20–29.

Grabosky, P., and G. Duffield. 2001. *Red Flags of Fraud.* Trends and Issues in Crime and Criminal Justice, Australian Institute of Criminology no. 200 (March). http://aic.gov.au/media_library/publications/tandi_pdf/tandi200.pdf.

Graham, B., and D. Dodd. 1934. *Security Analysis: The Classic 1934 Edition.* New York, NY: McGraw-Hill Trade, 1996.

Granger, C. 2005. "The Present and Future of Empirical Finance." *Financial Analysts Journal* 61 (4): 15–18.

Greer, R. 1997. "What Is an Asset Class, Anyway?" *Journal of Portfolio Management* 23 (2): 86–91.

Gregoriou, G., and F. Lhabitant. 2009. "Madoff: A Flock of Red Flags." *Journal of Wealth Management* 12 (1): 89–97.

Gruber, M. 1996. "Another Puzzle: The Growth in Activity Managed Mutual Funds." *Journal of Finance* 51 (3): 783–810.

Gupta, P. 2016. "Multi-Asset Investing in Asia Pacific: A Practitioner's Framework." CFA Conference Proceedings Quarterly 33 (2): 1–9.

Hanna, S., and P. Chen. 1997. "Subjective and Objective Risk Tolerance: Implications for Optimal Portfolios." *Financial Counseling and Planning* 8 (2): 17–26.

Hanna, S., and S. Lindamood. 2009. *Risk Tolerance: Cause or Effect?* Academy of Financial Services Conference Paper (January). www.researchgate.net/publication/279964280_Risk_Tolerance_Cause_or_Effect.

Harbron, G., D. Roberts, and J. Rowley. 2017. *The Case for Low-Cost Index-Fund Investing.* Vanguard Group (April). https://personal.vanguard.com/pdf/ISGIDX.pdf.

Harris, R., T. Jenkinson, and S. Kaplan. 2014. "Private Equity Performance: What Do We Know?" *Journal of Finance* 69 (5): 1851–1882.

Harvey, C., Liu, Y. and Zhu, H. 2016. "… and the Cross-Section of Expected Returns." *Review of Financial Studies* 29 (1): 5–68.

Hendricks, D., J. Patel, and R. Zeckhauser. 1993. "Hot Hands in Mutual Funds: Short-Run Persistence of Relative Performance, 1974–1988." *Journal of Finance* 48 (1): 93–130.

Hoyle, S. 2017. "CalPERS Says Consultants Could Do Better." Top1000funds.com (25 August). www.top1000funds.com/analysis/2017/08/25/calpers-says-consultants-could-do-better/.

Hsu, J., and V. Kalesnik. 2014. "Finding Smart Beta in the Factor Zoo." Research Affiliates Fundamentals (July). www.researchaffiliates.com/content/dam/ra/documents/Finding%20Smart%20Beta%20in%20the%20Factor%20Zoo_pdf.pdf.

Hudson-Wilson, S., J. Gordon, F. Fabozzi, M. Anson, and S. Giliberto. 2005. "Why Real Estate?" *Journal of Portfolio Management* 31 (5): 12–21.

Ibbotson, R., and P. Kaplan. 2000. "Does Asset Allocation Policy Explain 40, 90, or 100 Percent of Performance?" *Financial Analysts Journal* 56 (1): 26–33.

"Indecent Exposure: Markets Reveals the Good, the Bad and the Ugly." 2007. Staff Reporter, Market View, *Economist* (5 August). www.economist.com/node/9609521.

Institute of Internal Auditors. 2012. *International Standards for the Professional Practice of Internal Auditing.* IIA Standard (October). https://na.theiia.org/standards-guidance/Public%20Documents/IPPF%202013%20English.pdf.

———. 2013. *The Three Lines of Defense in Effective Risk Management and Control.* IIA position paper (January). www.iia.org.au/sf_docs/default-source/member-services/thethreelinesofdefenseineffectiveriskmanagementandcontrol_Position_Paper_Jan_2013.pdf?sfvrsn=0.

Jensen, M., and W. Meckling. 1976. "Theory of the Firm: Managerial Behavior, Agency Costs and Ownership Structure." *Journal of Financial Economics* 3 (4): 305–360. www.sfu.ca/~wainwrig/Econ400/jensen-meckling.pdf.

Jickling, M. 2009. *Barriers to Corporate Fraud.* New York: Nova Science.

Jorion, P. 2007. *Value at Risk: The New Benchmark for Managing Financial Risk.* New York: McGraw-Hill.

Kaplan, R., and D. Norton. 1992. "The Balanced Scorecard—Measures That Drive Performance." *Harvard Business Review* 70 (1): 71–79.

Kaplan, P., and L. Siegel. 1994. "Portfolio Theory Is Alive and Well." *Journal of Investing* 3 (3): 18–23.

Kay, J. 2016. *Other People's Money: The Real Business of Finance.* New York: Public Affairs.

Kentouris, C. 2017. *SEC's Liquidity Rule: How to Bucket Your Assets.* FinOps Report (16 August). https://finops.co/investments/secs-liquidity-rule-how-to-bucket-your-assets/.

Kraft, A., Vashishtha, R. and Venkatachalam, M. 2018. "Frequent Financial Reporting and Managerial Myopia." *Accounting Review* 93 (2): 249–275.

Leahy, S., and A. Drake. 2017. *FCA Challenges Status Quo for Asset Managers and Investment Consultants.* PWC Practice Note (June). www.pwc.co.uk/pensions/fca-status-quo-asset-managers-and-investment-consultants.html.

Lefevre, E. 1923. *Reminiscences of a Stock Operator.* New York: G.H. Doran.

Lhabitant, F. 2004. *Hedge Funds: Quantitative Insights.* Hoboken, NJ: Wiley.

———. 2017. *Portfolio Diversification*. London, UK: ISTE Press–Elsevier.

Lin, J. 2017. "Cutting Jobs, Street Repairs, Library Books to Keep Up with Pension Costs." *Los Angeles Times* (6 February). www.latimes.com/projects/la-le-me-richmond-pensions/.

Lo, A. 2008. "Efficient Markets Hypothesis." In *The New Palgrave Dictionary of Economics*, 2nd ed., ed. S. Durlauf and L. Blume, 1–17. London: Palgrave Macmillan.

Loewenstein, G., and R. Thaler. 1989. "Anomalies: Intertemporal Choice." *Journal of Economic Perspectives* 3 (4): 181–193.

Logue, D., and J. Rader. 1998. *Managing Pension Plans: A Comprehensive Guide to Improving Plan Performance*. Boston, MA: Harvard Business School Press.

Lusardi, A., and O. Mitchell. 2014. "The Economic Importance of Financial Literacy: Theory and Evidence." *Journal of Economic Literature* 52 (1): 5–44.

Lydenberg, S. 2011. *Investment Beliefs Statements*. IRI Working Paper, (30 January). http://iri.hks.harvard.edu/files/iri/files/iri_investment_beliefs_statements.pdf.

Malkiel, B. 1995. "Returns from Investing in Equity Mutual Funds 1971 to 1991." *Journal of Finance* 50 (2): 549–572.

———. 2012. "The Efficient-Market Hypothesis and the Financial Crisis." In *Rethinking the Financial Crisis*, ed. A. Blinder, A. Lo, and R. Solow, 75–98. New York: Russell Sage Foundation.

Malkiel, B., and C. Ellis. 2013. *The Elements of Investing: Easy Lessons for Every Investor*. New York: Wiley.

Mandelbrot, B. 1963. "The Variation of Certain Speculative Prices." *Journal of Business* 36 (4): 394–419.

———. 1967. "The Variation of Some Other Speculative Prices." *Journal of Business* 40 (4): 393–413.

Markowitz, H. 1952. "Portfolio Selection." *Journal of Finance* 7 (1): 77–91.

———. 1959. *Portfolio Selection: Efficient Diversification of Investment*. New York, NY: Wiley.

McCahery, J., Z. Sautner, and L. Starks. 2016. "Behind the Scenes: The Corporate Governance Preferences of Institutional Investors." *Journal of Finance* 71 (6): 2905–2932.

McKenzie, C., M. Liersch, and S. Finkelstein. 2006. "Recommendations Implicit in Policy Defaults." *Psychological Science* 17 (5): 414–420.

McMenamin, S. 2015. Guidance for Investment Committees Is Overdue. Pensions & Investments (5 March). www.pionline.com/article/20150305/ONLINE/150309968/guidance-for-investment-committees-is-overdue.

Merton, R. 1973. "An Intertemporal Capital Asset Pricing Model." *Econometrica* 41 (5): 867–887.

———. 1997. *Applications of Option-Pricing Theory: Twenty-Five Years Later.* Nobel Lecture (9 December). http://nobelprize.org/nobel_prizes/economics/laureates/1997/merton-lecture.pdf.

———. 2007. "The Future of Retirement Planning." In *The Future of Life-Cycle Saving and Investing*, ed. Z. Bodie, D. McLeavey, and L. Siegel, 5–14. Charlottesville, VA: Research Foundation of the CFA Institute.

Milevsky, M. 2009. *Are You a Stock or a Bond? Create Your Own Pension Plan for a Secure Financial Future.* Upper Saddle River, NJ: FT Press.

———. 2010. *Your Money Milestones.* Upper Saddle River, NJ: FT Press.

———. 2012. *The 7 Most Important Equations for Your Retirement.* Mississauga, ON: Wiley Canada.

Milevsky, M., and A. Macqueen. 2010. *Pensionize Your Nest Egg.* Mississauga, ON: Wiley Canada.

Milevsky, M., and K. Song. 2010. "Do Markets Like Frozen Defined Benefit Pensions? An Event Study." *Journal of Risk and Insurance* 77 (4): 893–909.

Mitchell, O., and A. Lusardi, eds. 2011. *Financial Literacy: Implications for Retirement Security and the Financial Marketplace.* Oxford, UK: Oxford University Press.

Mitchell, O., and J. Turner. 2010. "Human Capital Risk and Pension Outcomes." In *Evaluating the Financial Performance of Pension Funds*, ed. R. Hinz, P. Antolín, R. Heinz, and J. Yermo, 119–151. Washington, DC: World Bank.

Mitchell, O., R. Maurer, and B. Hammond, eds. 2014. *Recreating Sustainable Retirement: Resilience, Solvency, and Tail Risk.* Oxford, UK: Oxford University Press.

Mongars, P., and C. Marchal-Dombrat. 2006. "Commodities: An Asset Class in Their Own Right?" *Financial Stability Review* (9): 31–38.

Mooney, A. "Growing Number of Pension Funds Divest from Fossil Fuels." 2017. *Financial Times* (28 April). www.ft.com/content/fe88b788-29ad-11e7-9ec8-168383da43b7.

MSCI. 2015. *MSCI Diversified Multiple Factor Indexes Methodology*. MSCI Index Methodology (September). www.msci.com/eqb/methodology/meth_docs/MSCI_Diversified_Multiple_Factor_Indexes_Methodology_September_2015.pdf.

Munnell, A., and S. Sass. 2008. *Working Longer: The Answer to the Retirement Income Crisis*. Washington, DC: Brookings Institution.

Munro, J., and M. Pagnozzi. 2017. *The Compliance Investment: Realising the Value of Compliance through Greater Effectiveness, Efficiency, and Sustainability*. KPMG Insights (March). https://home.kpmg.com/au/en/home/insights/2017/03/compliance-investment.html.

Natixis Global Asset Management. 2017. 2017 Global Retirement Index. (July). https://ngam.natixis.com/us/resources/2017-global-retirement-index.

Neal, D., and G. Warren. 2015. "Long-Term Investing as an Agency Problem." CIFR Paper No. 063/2015 (July). www.ifswf.org/sites/default/files/Publications/Long-Term_Investing_as_an_Agency_Problem.pdf.

Newell, G., A. De Francesco, and H. W. Peng. 2011. "The Performance of Unlisted Infrastructure in Portfolios." *Journal of Property Research* 28 (1): 59–74.

Newell, R. 2017. *Is Listed Infra Really Worth It?* Fund Selector Asia (22 August). www.fundselectorasia.com/news/1037625/listed-infra-worth.

Oberhofer, G. 2001. Hedge Funds: A New Asset Class or Just a Change in Perspective? *Alternative Investment Management Association Newsletter* (December). www.aima.org/uploads/2001/Dec/frankrussell.pdf.

OECD. 2009. "OECD Guidelines for Pension Fund Governance." Organisation for Economic Co-operation and Development (5 June). www.oecd.org/finance/private-pensions/34799965.pdf.

———. 2014. *Risk Management and Corporate Governance, Corporate Governance*. Paris: OECD Publishing.

Paul, S., and D. Kurtz. 2013. *Managing Conflicts of Interest*. Washington, DC: BoardSource.

Pfeffer, J., R. Cialdini, B. Hanna, and K. Knopoff. 1998. "Faith in Supervision and the Self-Enhancement Bias: Two Psychological Reasons Why Managers Don't Empower Workers." *Basic and Applied Social Psychology* 20 (4): 313–321.

Pompian, M. 2017. *Risk Profiling through a Behavioral Finance Lens.* Charlottesville, VA: CFA Institute Research Foundation.

Qantas Airways Limited. 2017. Route Maps: Domestic Australia and New Zealand (21 September). www.qantas.com/travel/airlines/route-maps/global/en.

Rachev, S., S. Stoyanov, and F. Fabozzi. 2008. *Advanced Stochastic Models, Risk Assessment, and Portfolio Optimization.* Hoboken, NJ: Wiley.

Rahaim, C. 2005. *The Fiduciary: An In-depth Guide to Fiduciary Duties—From Studebaker to Enron.* New York: iUniverse.

Rengifo, E., R. Trendafilov, and E. Trifan. 2014. "Behavioral Portfolio Theory and Investment Management." In *Investor Behavior: The Psychology of Financial Planning and Investing,* ed. H. Baker and V. Ricciardi, 421–438. Hoboken, NJ: Wiley.

Rice, M., R. DiMeo, and M. Porter. 2012. *Nonprofit Asset Management: Effective Investment Strategies and Oversight.* New York: Wiley.

Richey, G. 2016. "Sin Is In: An Alternative to Socially Responsible Investing." *Journal of Investing* 25 (2): 136–143.

Rittenberg, L., and F. Martens. 2012. Enterprise Risk Management—Understanding and Communicating Risk Appetite. Committee of Sponsoring Organizations of the Treadway Commission, Thought Leadership in ERM (January). www.coso.org/Documents/ERM-Understanding-and-Communicating-Risk-Appetite.pdf.

Rothballer, C., and C. Kaserer. 2011. "The Risk Profile of Infrastructure Investments: Challenging Conventional Wisdom." *Journal of Structured Finance* 18 (2): 95–109.

Salazar, Y., R. Bianchi, M. Drew, and S. Trück. 2017. "The Diversification Delta: A Different Perspective." *Journal of Portfolio Management* 43 (4): 112–124.

Samuelson, P. 1965. "Proof That Properly Anticipated Prices Fluctuate Randomly." *Industrial Management Review* 6 (2): 41–49.

Santoli, M. 2017. *Get Ready for Dramatically Lower Stock Market Returns over the Next Decade.* CBNC.com (7 May). www.cnbc.com/2017/05/07/get-ready-for-dramatically-lower-stock-market-returns-over-the-next-decade.html.

Scharfman, J. 2015. *Hedge Fund Governance: Evaluating Oversight, Independence, and Conflicts.* San Diego, CA: Elsevier.

Schaus, S. 2010. *Designing Successful Target-Date Strategies for Defined Contribution Plans*. Hoboken, NJ: Wiley.

Schaus, S., and Y. Gao. 2017. *Successful Defined Contribution Investment Design*. Hoboken, NJ: Wiley.

Scott, B., J. Balsamo, K. McShane, and C. Tasopoulos. 2017. *The Global Case for Strategic Asset Allocation and an Examination of Home Bias*. Vanguard Group (February). https://personal.vanguard.com/pdf/ISGGAA.pdf.

Sexauer, S., and L. Siegel. 2017. "Floods and Deserts: Why the Dream of a Secure Pension for Everyone Is Still Unattained." *Journal of Retirement* 4 (4): 12–24.

Sharpe, W. 1966. "Mutual Fund Performance." *Journal of Business* 39 (S1): 119–138.

Siegel, L. 2015. "After 70 Years of Fruitful Research, Why Is There Still a Retirement Crisis?" *Financial Analysts Journal* 71 (1): 6–15.

Siegel, L., and S. Sexauer. 2017. "Five Mysteries Surrounding Low and Negative Interest Rates." *Journal of Portfolio Management* 43 (3): 77–86.

Smith, A. (1759) 2016. *The Theory of Moral Sentiments*. Create Space Independent Publishing Platform. London: A. Millar.

———. (1776) 1937. *An Inquiry into the Nature and Causes of the Wealth of Nations*. New York: The Modern Library.

Smith, M. 2016. "What's Eating Asset Consultants?" *FINSIA InFinance* (2 June). http://finsia.com/insights/news/news-article/2016/06/02/what-s-eating-asset-consultants.

Sortino, F. 2010. *The Sortino Framework for Constructing Portfolios: Focusing on Desired Target Return to Optimize Upside Potential Relative to Downside Risk*. Amsterdam: Elsevier.

Sortino, F., and L. Price. 1994. "Performance Measurement in a Downside Risk Framework." *Journal of Investing* 3 (3): 59–64.

Southwell, P. 2017. "Listed Infrastructure's Real Role—And It's Not Fake." *Financial Times* (31 July). www.ft.com/content/4bb41710-72eb-11e7-93ff-99f383b09ff9.

Spaulding, D. 1997. *Measuring Investment Performance: Calculating and Evaluating Investment Risk and Return*. New York: McGraw-Hill.

————. 2003. *Investment Performance Attribution: A Guide to What It Is, How to Calculate It, and How to Use It*. New York: McGraw-Hill.

State Street Global Services. 2014. *The Future of Investment Compliance for Asset Owners: The Next Great Transformation*. Global Services, State Street Corporation (December). www.statestreet.com/content/dam/statestreet/documents/Articles/TheFutureofInvComplianceforAO.pdf.

Statman, M. 2001. "How Important Is Asset Allocation?" *Journal of Asset Management* 2 (2): 128–135.

Stein, J. 1989. "Efficient Capital Markets, Inefficient Firms: A Model of Myopic Corporate Behavior." *Quarterly Journal of Economics* 104 (4): 655–669.

Strangeland, D., and H. Turtle. 1999. "Time Diversification: Fact or Fallacy." *Journal of Financial Education* 25 (2): 1–13.

Sunit, S. 2014. *The Principal–Agent Problem in Finance*. Charlottesville, VA: CFA Institute Research Foundation. www.cfapubs.org/doi/pdf/10.2470/rflr.v9.n1.1.

Taleb, N. 2004. *Fooled by Randomness: The Hidden Role of Chance in Life and in the Markets*, 2nd ed. New York: Thomson Texere.

————. 2007. *The Black Swan*. London, UK: Penguin Books.

Tan Bhala, K., R. Yeh, and W. Bhala. 2016. *International Investment Management: Theory, Ethics and Practice*. London, UK: Routledge.

Telser, L. 1955. "Safety First and Hedging." *Review of Economic Studies* 23 (1): 1–16.

Thaler, R. 1980. "Toward a Positive Theory of Consumer Choice." *Journal of Economic Behavior & Organization* 1 (1): 39–60.

Tilles, S. 1963. "How to Evaluate Corporate Strategy." *Harvard Business Review* 41 (4): 111–121.

Tipple, B. 2010. "Avoiding the Pitfalls: Best Practices in Manager Research and Due Diligence." *CFA Institute Conference Proceedings Quarterly* 27 (2): 46–51.

Urwin, R., S. Breban, T. Hodgson, and A. Hunt. 2001. "Risk Budgeting in Pension Investment." *British Actuarial Journal* 7 (3): 319–347.

USA Mutuals. 2017. *The Vice Fund: Fund Update* (June). www.usamutuals.com/pdf/fsb0.nschmidt.xf00.195964.vf_fact_sheet.pdf.

Van de Venter, G., D. Michayluk, and G. Davey. 2012. "A Longitudinal Study of Financial Risk Tolerance." *Journal of Economic Psychology* 33 (4): 794–800.

Vermorken, M., F. Medda, and F. Schröder. 2012. "The Diversification Delta: A Higher-Moment Measure for Portfolio Diversification." *Journal of Portfolio Management* 39 (1): 67–74.

Vernon, S. 2012. *Money for Life*. Oxnard, CA: Rest-of-Life Communications.

von Moltke, Helmuth, the Elder. (1871) 1971. *Strategy Its Theory and Application*. Westport, CT: Greenwood.

Walsh, M. 2016. *Dallas Stares Down a Texas-Size Threat of Bankruptcy.* Dealbook, *New York Times* (30 November). www.nytimes.com/2016/11/21/business/dealbook/dallas-pension-debt-threat-of-bankruptcy.html?mcubz=1.

Waring, M. Barton. 2011. *Pension Finance: Putting the Risks and Costs of the Defined Benefit Plan Back under Your Control*. Hoboken, NJ: John Wiley & Sons.

Waring, B., and L. Siegel. 2005. "Debunking Some Myths of Active Management." *Journal of Investing* 14 (2): 20–28.

Watson, A. 1991. *Legal Origins and Legal Change*. London: Hambledon Press.

Watson Wyatt. 2004. *Remapping*. Reigate, UK: Watson Wyatt.

———. 2006. *Changing Lanes*. Reigate, UK: Watson Wyatt.

Wermers, R. 2000. "Mutual Fund Performance: An Empirical Decomposition into Stock-Picking Talent, Style, Transactions Costs, and Expenses." *Journal of Finance* 55 (4): 1655–1695.

White, Amanda. 2017. "Björn Kvarnskog: Taking Stock at the Future Fund." *Investment Magazine* (26 September). https://investmentmagazine.com.au/2017/09/bjorn-kvarnskog-taking-stock-at-the-future-fund/.

Wilkinson, L. 2017) *Defined Benefits: Valuing and Managing Liabilities*. PPI Briefing Note Number 93 (March). www.uk.mercer.com/content/dam/mercer/attachments/europe/uk/uk-2017-defined-benefits-valuing-and-managing-liabilities.pdf.

Williams, K., and S. Cornelius. 2016. "The Asset Owners' Conundrum: Insourcing of Asset Management." *Performance Magazine* (September). https://www2.deloitte.com/content/dam/Deloitte/lu/Documents/financial-services/performancemagazine/articles/lu_asset-owner-conundrum-092016.pdf.

Williams, R. 2017. "Make or Buy: What's Really Transforming the Superannuation Value Chain." Parametric Portfolio Associates Working Paper (February). www.ioandc.com/wp-content/uploads/2017/02/6-Insource-outsource-paper.pdf.

Willis Towers Watson. 2017a. *Global Pension Assets Study 2017* (30 January). www.willistowerswatson.com/en/insights/2017/01/global-pensions-asset-study-2017.

———. 2017b. *The World's 300 Largest Pension Funds—Year Ended 2016* (4 September). www.willistowerswatson.com/en-TH/insights/2017/09/The-worlds-300-largest-pension-funds-year-ended-2016.

Wojcik, D., E. Knight, and V. Pazitka. 2018. "What Turns Cities into International Financial Centres? Analysis of Cross-Border Investment Banking 2000–2014." *Journal of Economic Geography* 18 (1): 1–33.

Wojcik, D., D. MacDonald-Korth, and S. Zhao. 2016. "The Political-Economic Geography of Foreign Exchange Trading." *Journal of Economic Geography* 17 (2): 267–286.

Woods, C., and R. Urwin. 2010. "Putting Sustainable Investing into Practice: A Governance Framework for Pension Funds." *Journal of Business Ethics* 92 (S1): 1–19.

World Bank. 2008. "The World Bank Pension Conceptual Framework." World Bank Pension Reform Primer (September). http://siteresources.worldbank.org/INTPENSIONS/Resources/395443-1121194657824/PRPNoteConcept_Sept2008.pdf.

World Economic Forum. 2017. We'll Live to 100—How Can We Afford It? (May). www3.weforum.org/docs/WEF_White_Paper_We_Will_Live_to_100.pdf.

Xiong, J., and T. Idzorek. 2011. "The Impact of Skewness and Fat Tails on the Asset Allocation Decision." *Financial Analysts Journal* 67 (2): 23–35.

Yao, R., S. Hanna, and S. Lindamood. 2004. "Changes in Financial Risk Tolerance, 1983–2001." *Financial Services Review* 13 (4): 249–266.

Young, S. 2007. "Fiduciary Duties as a Helpful Guide to Ethical Decision-Making in Business." *Journal of Business Ethics* 74 (1): 1–15.

Named Endowments

The CFA Institute Research Foundation acknowledges with sincere gratitude the generous contributions of the Named Endowment participants listed below.

Gifts of at least US$100,000 qualify donors for membership in the Named Endowment category, which recognizes in perpetuity the commitment toward unbiased, practitioner-oriented, relevant research that these firms and individuals have expressed through their generous support of the CFA Institute Research Foundation.

Senior Research Fellows

Financial Services Analyst Association

For more on upcoming Research Foundation publications and webcasts, please visit www.cfainstitute.org/learning/foundation.